OF PRISON,
PERVERSIONS AND
EXECUTIONS

OF PRISON, PERVERSIONS AND EXECUTIONS

✦

BEHIND THE WIRE: An Inside Look at the prison system from one who lived it.

Richard K. Minard

iUniverse, Inc.

New York Lincoln Shanghai

OF PRISON, PERVERSIONS AND EXECUTIONS
BEHIND THE WIRE: An Inside Look at the prison system from one who lived it.

iUniverse books may be ordered through booksellers or by contacting:

iUniverse
2021 Pine Lake Road, Suite 100
Lincoln, NE 68512
www.iuniverse.com
1-800-Authors (1-800-288-4677)

ISBN-13: 978-0-595-33457-5 (pbk)
ISBN-13: 978-0-595-66943-1 (cloth)
ISBN-13: 978-0-595-78253-6 (ebk)
ISBN-10: 0-595-33457-1 (pbk)
ISBN-10: 0-595-66943-3 (cloth)
ISBN-10: 0-595-78253-1 (ebk)

Printed in the United States of America

This book is dedicated to my wife Kathleen. My partner in life.

Contents

HOW IT BEGAN

Most of my life I've been interested in crime and criminals. As a kid I was a petty criminal. My older brother Lenny—dead now 30 yrs.—schooled me on crime, to an extent, but most I learned on my own. My earliest memories of my criminal leanings are about when I stole a quarter out of my mothers' purse so I could go to the pharmacy downstairs and buy a snickers bar and some Chiclets. I ate them as fast as possible and hid the change in a drainpipe. I was four going on five when this incident took place. We moved from over the pharmacy when I was five years old. The move didn't curtail my criminal activities.

The neighborhood I spent the next 12 yrs. in was what you would call dysfunctional. At least the people I hung around with were dysfunctional. We experimented with all sorts of drugs, committed petty crimes and basically did what we wanted. I fancied myself a criminal. When the Godfather movie came out, one of my favorites, I fantasized that I was as powerful as the characters in the film. I associated crime with power.

My brother Lenny and I spent the night with my grandma and grandpa on occasion. My grandma had true crime magazines at her house and my brother and I would devour them. We would spend hours reading them. The covers were great. They displayed buxom women in submissive positions. An enraged man holding a weapon—usually a knife—menaced threatened and tore at their clothes. I wanted to be that man. I had a child's skewed sense of power coupled with a raging libido.

I never committed a crime that had a face attached to it. No one I grew up with ever did. We were shits but we never physically hurt anyone. We were dysfunctional not ruthless. We were selfish but we had a sense of self. At that time I was fascinated by people/criminals that were raised in an environment that had instilled a deep sense of hate and self-loathing in them. The other class of criminal that interested me were the ones with no conscience. Most people behind bars are a bit of both. My first taste of these types of people came when I was 16 yrs. old. Like I said, I and most of my friends were petty criminals and it caught up to me one day after some guns were stolen in a burglary. I was really high and had some drugs on me when a cop just happened to enter the alley I was walking down. He stopped me and I got pissed and hit him. Very, very stupid. It was, I believe October. I was taken to the juvenile detention center where they got a court order to fingerprint me. My prints turned up on one of the guns that were recovered. Several more were missing and they wanted them back. I had to stay in detention until after January 22nd—my 17th birthday. I was allowed out only when I agreed to live with my aunt and uncle outside the city limits.

During my time in detention I met many like-minded kids but some I met were real criminals. A real criminal has no empathy. He thinks only of himself no matter what the situation or familial con-nection. For example, a criminal that is a father does not love his wife or son or daughter. He may say he does but he doesn't. Love does not exist within him, period. Many people in prison are like this. Some of the kids I met in juvy were like this. They had relatives in prison, usually a father or uncle, mother or grandparent, and cousins, usually more than one. They were raised to be criminals. These were the ones that raped the younger, weaker kids. They were malicious, they were hate filled. One I remember was Buddy Love. He told me that the only thing he remembered about his dad was being told "Only a graveyard or prison holds a Love." Buddy was fulfilling his father's demand.

After my brush with the juvenile authorities I decided to clean up my act. Since I'd dropped out of school in the 9th grade all I could get were shit jobs. I started working on loading docks. I injured my back in an accident that made it impossible to work on the dock any longer. Through Vocational Rehabilitation I went to school. In January 1995 I graduated with a degree in Criminology and Criminal Justice.

My first job was in the Juvenile Justice System. This job was a learning experience. It taught me a lot and confirmed some of the opinions I'd formed while in school. It's long been my opinion that poor parenting is at the root of juvenile crime. In my personal experience it was the fact that my parents were overwhelmed. I am one of ten children. I've always had a combative nature and the constant fight was draining on my parents. They made an unconscious decision that if I was going to break the law I would have to pay. This was an extremely dangerous decision. Interacting with the parents of the kids confined confirmed my opinion. Juvenile crime is the parent's fault, to a point. If you don't have the stamina don't have kids. Too many children are born to parents that have no sense in how to raise them. In times past whole communities took on the task but that rarely happens today.

By the time I received my degree I had been steeped in criminology. What was an interest had become my avocation. What I wanted more than anything was to work maximum security in an institution that had death row. I got my wish. While going to school I wrote a letter to the corrections department head asking to be put on the list of states witnesses to an execution. I received a reply that said they received my letter. My wife and I drove out to the prison one day just to look at it while I was still in school. Quite an imposing structure, more razor wire than I saw my whole time in the military. Potosi Correctional Center.—P.C.C.—Most of what I knew about Potosi I read about in the newspaper. I always kept up with the latest execution. Death row was now at Potosi, it was formerly at Jefferson City Correctional Center. P.C.C had an escape. Dennis Kirksey escaped one rainy morning by going under a fence and then stealing a car that an employee had left the keys in. No conspiracy just dumb luck. The area is under surveillance now and is known as "Kirkseys hole".

I was familiar with the Potosi area which is the seat of government in Washington county. For years I went deer hunting in the national forest that is just outside Potosi. Mining was the chief economic foundation of the county and surrounding counties for many years. Over time the mines played out and the county needed a shot in the arm. The shot came in the form of Potosi Correctional Center.

I applied for the position of corrections caseworker and in June 1995 I was granted an interview. During the interview I was asked if I knew when an inmate was lying. Figuring to gain some insight into the criminal way of thinking I said no. When he moves his lips was the response and the interviewers started laughing. Such is the prevailing attitude. I started work there in July. With my education and lifetime experiences I thought I had an understanding of the job. It is impossible to prepare yourself for this kind of job.

A corrections caseworker is the frontline administrative position. You are literally the caseworker for a group of inmates. The contact that you have with the inmate population is the most personal. Corrections officers—guards—supervise and make sure the bad people stay away from the good people i.e. do not escape.

Caseworkers have to listen to the inmates. We have to make sure that they receive what the courts have promised them. We have to talk to their relatives and friends. We have to know their histories through their file material.

An inmates file is off limits to all but a select few. Everything in it is confidential. The inmate is never allowed to view it. This pisses off the inmates to no end. Their way of thinking is that it is "their" file and they should be able to view it. It's the states file.

I was to learn that inmates care about one thing—themselves. On my first day I walked in dressed like a professional. Suit and tie. I introduced myself and was told to remove the tie. An opportunistic inmate has the tool to strangle you I was told. Even as a caseworker I had to get "suited up" to go inside. We all carried a radio, keys to many doors, pepper spray, handcuffs and rubber gloves. Standard issue. I had to go through seven doors to get to my office. Maximum security prisons are maze like. For the first couple of weeks you are a bit disoriented. My new co-workers somewhat playfully took bets on how long I would last. My supervisor called me into the office at the end of my first day and and asked quite seriously if I was going to return tomorrow. Many people don't return after the first day. I assured her I would.

Working in a maximum security prison has got to be one of the most stressful jobs there is. Most of the inmate population is sentenced to death, life without parole, life with parole or with a sentence longer than twenty years. If you are not in that category then you are so out of control that by accumulating enough "write-ups" you can only be held in maximum security. Some of these are the worst. I have since had the opportunity to work in lower level institutions where all of the sentences are parolable. No comparison.

One of the first things I learned about Potosi is that although we had all of the inmates that had been sentenced to death in the state of Missouri there was no death row. Dora Schriro, the director, had decided within months of my arriving that death row was unnecessary. When the decision was made it was not without much controversy. I was told that officials from Texas had contacted some staff at the prison and warned that blood would run from one end of the prison to the other if they let them out into population. It never happened. Dora Schriro had decided and rightly so that the only difference between a death sentence and say someone sentenced to life without was the sentence itself. For every death row inmate there are many inmates that committed the same type or worse crime. To say it is reserved for the most heinous is bullshit.

The most heinous crime ever committed is the psychological and physical abuse a child must endure at the hands of the parent. The only protector a child senses is the parent and when the parent becomes the torturer there can be no worse crime. Check out death rows throughout the states and see how many parents are on death row.

The inmates that had been on death row were not pleased. While segregated they'd had single man cells. General population had been double bunked for some time. The thought of sharing a cell caused some to check into administrative segregation—the hole.

Capital punishment—death sentence—inmates are almost completely preoccupied with their cases. The amount of paperwork they have is staggering. They do not want to play the games that they have to in population. They don't want to be bothered. Too bad. Some population inmates refused to be bunked with c.p.'s. Society has made them out to be boogy men and inmates are a selfish bunch. Those that refused went to the hole. Other states still have death row. It's a waste of taxpayer dollars-added security and special handling—and actually benefits the c.p. inmate.

The volatility of my surroundings revealed itself within my first week. Unfortunately I was the cause. At Potosi we practiced controlled movement. Only a small number of inmates could be moving at one time. During meals for example only one walk of one wing of one house would eat at a time. Timing is important. I had stepped outside on the yard during one of these chow movements. I was standing next to my housing unit observing the movement when an inmate asked if he could speak with me. Being inexperienced I said O. K.. One inmate turned into two. Two turned into four and pretty soon I was surrounded by a half dozen or so. Two things I want to point out. As a caseworker my decisions supercede the controlled movement. If I pull an inmate out of movement no one will question me. Also, if one inmate see's another getting some sort of preferential treatment—say being pulled out of a controlled movement—they automatically figure they are entitled to the same treatment. Without permission. I had a lot to learn. The inmate I was talking to started to back away from me as did the others. As soon as I sensed what was happening I heard a painful smack. Two inmates behind me—that hated each other—had met up on the walk due to me holding up the movement. As I said timing is every-thing. As soon as the fight began most of the inmates on the walk stopped to watch creating a worse situation. The officers that were controlling the movement now had a fight to break up. They also had to keep the movement going. Most demands from the officers to keep moving were ignored by the inmates. I got into the office and reported the fight. The other caseworkers almost knocked me down getting out to the walk. I followed back outside thinking I was going in the wrong direction. Pepper spray was everywhere. The officers had the fighters cuffed and were on their way to medical. As soon as the pepper spray hit the air the inmates that stopped to watch started hustling to get off the walk quickly.

By the time I got back outside to where it all started it was over. I was amazed. It started and was over with in less than ten minutes. I found out that anytime a code is called on the radio for a fight, stab-bing or officer in need of assistance every available person no matter what your position responds. Staff overwhelms the situation if possi-ble.

One of the most demanding parts of the job as caseworker is office hours. Three days a week six hours a day the inmates can come to your office and complain. They don't come in to thank you for doing a wonderful job. It's during these sessions that you get to know the inmate.

In inmate think anything that impacts them negatively is a crisis that must be fixed now. A disagreement with their celly must be handled with a cell change. Inmates ask for cell changes all the time. The top reason for a cell change request is racial. Sometimes a white and black inmate end up celled together. Even if the inmates themselves are O.K. with the situation—a rare event—other inmates will not tolerate it. A white man celling with a black man is a no no. The state supports this integration. They almost have to. To deny a cell change because of race will guarantee a fight no one knows at what level. So it makes sense to approve it and keep the peace. The only real exception to this unwritten rule are the pimps or stable bosses. These are exclusively black men that victimize usually young weak white inmates. On rare occasions a young weak black inmate is victimized. In Missouri it is pretty rare to have Asian or Hispanic inmates but those minorities are equally victimized. Pimps are incredibly violent. They have to be. Or they must be charismatic enough or wealthy enough to have muscle. Muscle is other inmates doing the fighting for the pimps. I was asked once if homosexuality/rape really occurred in prison. Not only does it occur it is used for sport, it is a commodity. The people that run the prisons know this and do almost nothing to try and stop it. There are homosexuals in prison but they are a rare occurrence.

Let me describe the rape situation. Pimps look for the inmate that most resembles a woman. If you come to prison and are small, young and thin and have little facial hair you will be not only raped but made a part of a stable. Unless you want to live in the hole.

Pimps have so many ways to manipulate and are not getting out anytime soon so they have plenty of time to "turn" someone. If you come to prison and are big, fat and hairy you probably won't be approached. Some inmates arrive ready to be manipulated. It was during office hours that I first met T-Cup. The reason I call him T-Cup has to do with a play on his name and that he was fragile like china. He had been in my housing unit for about three or four days. His file finally showed up on my desk—better late than never—and he was in on a murder charge. He had befriended a family through his church. In the family there was a young boy. He molested the boy, the boy threatened to tell so he cut the boys throat. The inmate rumor was that he cut the boys head off. Almost but not quite. An inmate in this situation gets no protection. Even though he was white the Aryans wouldn't touch him. Had he come in with almost any other charge he might have been able to turn to the whites for protection. But not for this. Before T-Cup arrived at my office I got a call from one of the housing unit officers and he told me that a well known pimp had already befriended T-Cup. It was their belief that T-Cup was raped that day. I was expecting an upset young man that had recently been violated what I got was a request from T-Cup to cell with the pimp. I asked him why he wanted to cell with this guy and I warned him that this guy has a reputation of victimizing others. He explained to me that he knew that his choice was the rest of his life in the hole or try to make it in population. He didn't want to live in the hole. I asked him if he knew that he would have to put out with anybody the pimp told him to. He told me he did and was O.K. with it. Cell change denied. My boss overrode my decision in order to be fair. He told me that when we catch the pimp with his dick in T-Cups ass we could separate them but for now they could cell together. Later I found out that T-Cup had aids. You can't protect them from themselves.

Rape inside of prison is only one of the horrors that you must get used to if you work in prison. I personally found it to be the most horrible. If an inmate resists it turns into the prison saying "Shit on my dick or blood on my blade, you decide." Unfortunately, there is no shortage of meat for the rapist. So many young men who have no clue what really awaits. So few who have the strength to take the assaults if not willing to bend over. But there are some. Joe was one. He and two friends got drunk and got into a fight with a man who was also drunk. One witness reported that Joe said I'll kill you. The next day the man was found dead. He was found at the bottom of a well that had been abandoned and partially covered. Joe swore he didn't do it. Long story short the courts didn't believe him. He was sentenced to twenty five to life. Joe was short and stocky. He was raised on a farm and he was tough. I received a call from my supervisor to go talk to Joe in the infirmary. When I saw him his face resembled hamburger. I had never seen anyone beaten so bad. I asked him what happened. He told me he fell out of his bunk. He demanded to be released from the infirmary. I asked the nurse if the infirmary was going to hold him she said "of course not what do you think, is this a hospital? We all laughed including Joe and he was released. He wore his bruises like a badge. A couple of months passed Joe was assaulted again though not as bad. He refused to say anything. He refused to go into protective custody. Then one day there was a radio call for a stabbing in the gym. They had a victim—a pimp—but no one saw the assault. The pimp claimed he didn't see who stabbed him. I called Joe into my office just to talk. I asked him among other things if he had any idea who may have done the stabbing. He didn't know but said he thought someone was probably just trying to make a point. The respect Joe got from the other white inmates protected him from further problems. As far as I know Joe was not bothered again. Most don't have his resolve. This is the reality of prison. Those individuals who talk about getting tough on crime I would love for them to listen to a young man getting raped. Some are raped so brutally and so often their sphincter muscle weakens and they have a hard time holding their bowels. Listening to the nurses talk they have to issue adult diapers for some.

For every inmate there is a story. In maximum security there are no dull days. After awhile you get used to working with inmates. The atmosphere is so highly charged that after a while chaos is normal.

I had not been working at the prison long when I experienced my first lockdown and search. I came to work like normal but when I got to the admin. offices most of the staff that should have been inside already were in the training room. The evening before there had been a stabbing in the gym. They got the shank-knife—and it was made out of a piece of stainless steel coat hook. The way it was made there could have been more shanks made from it. The inmate lived and had no idea why he was targeted. We had to find the rest of the coat hook. We would spend the rest of the day searching every square inch of the prison. The warden contacted other prisons to get more help. These lockdown searches happen frequently. During lockdown nothing else happens. The inmates are fed in there cells. No one moves. The officers search and also remove everything from the cell. My job is to record everything taken in the hopes that the inmate will get his property back. Maybe. One inmate in particular was upset that his court material would be destroyed. When I walked to his cell to try to assure him that we wouldn't destroy his court material he said he wanted to show me what he was talking about. He produced 8x10 color photos of an autopsy being performed. They were of his mother. He stabbed her to death. He liked to show his photos to see what kind of reaction he could get. Somehow they got lost during the search. I'm sure he wrote to his lawyer to get some more. Like I said for every inmate there is a story. So many inmates and so many stories that they start to blur. You deal in tragedy like a mechanic deals in cars. It is the exceptional inmate that burns himself into your memory. One inmate in particular sticks out because of his personality.

I consider myself a scientist. I am an agnostic and have no belief system therefore the concept of evil—a belief system—escapes me. I met many bad men in prison but they are just that, bad. My main focus after I had been there about six months was to work the execution detail. While in school I had done a lot of research work on executions and different forms of punishment. I wanted to find out for myself if I could watch a man be executed and what my reaction would be. I also wanted to know what went on behind the scenes. First I had to write to the execution coordinator-a caseworker like myself—and volunteer my services. Next I was interviewed to see what position I might work well in. In the short time I had been working at PCC I had gained the reputation of being highly professional. Because of this it was decided that I would work as an assistant to the execution coordinator and as a witness escort. I would be escorting one of four groups. The department director and division director had to be escorted. The states witnesses had to be escorted. These usually consisted of prosecuting attorneys, police, press people or other interested persons with connections to get in. The condemned has witnesses and these include clergy or spiritual adviser, family or friends. Then there are the victims witnesses. This group gets the most attention from the department. This is the group I usually worked with.

Prior to working my first execution I was inundated with information from people that had already worked an execution. Some of it relevant information and some just stories about executions past. Working an execution is one of the most nervwracking events there is. For some a sense of humor is what is used to cut the tension. The institutional investigators office maintains the monitors in the death cell and areas surrounding it. They make sure that all of the official duties are finished. Time of death recording, collection of the ekg tape and signing off on the death certificate are just some of their duties. During one execution they were short their secretary so they got a volunteer to help out. She was nervous the whole time. She didn't want anything to go wrong. The investigators didn't help. Knowing how nervous she was they started increasing her anxiety. Files governing the execution were misplaced. They would send her to find things that they needed only to determine they weren't really needed. They had her drained by the time the execution was over. As the last act they all went to the execution chamber. The deceased was still on the gurney. They told her that when a man is executed his penis gets hard, harder than it ever has in his life and one of their last official duties is to measure the deceased penis. They then brought out a tape measure and handed it to her. When she absolutely refused to touch the deceased they all started laughing. Like I said some use humor to cut the tension. Each execution is different. The circumstances behind the execution usually sets the tone. It shouldn't but it does. The inmate himself, his personality and the crime for which he is now being executed all comes into play. It doesn't change anything. He's still going to die but the tension is different. A good example is the execution of Bannister. While incarcerated he was a royal pain in the ass. Typical selfish inmate to the nth degree. He was the type that would not go gently into that good night. Like I said most C.P. inmates are so busy with their cases that just to be left alone is fine with them. Others, like Bannister, are so full of hate and so pissed off that they are going to be executed that their lives evolve around fucking with anyone they can. The numbers of frivolous grievances that they file is incredible. Some of them will file grievances for almost every encounter that they have with staff members. This causes an enormous amount of stress on staff members that cannot maintain their objectivity. Banisters wife was from Europe. Great Britain I believe. She had people from all over the world contacting the prison on his behalf. The Pope sent word that execution was wrong and that his execution as well as others should not be carried out. Some staff thought his sentence would be reduced because he had a world wide following. On the night of Banisters execution people were happy. People who never took a drink in their lives toasted his death. Like I said each execution is different.

The following stories are all true. From July 1995 until July 2002 I worked at Potosi Correctional Center and Farmington Correctional Center. I have witnessed over twenty executions. I have had the unique opportunity of working with minimum security inmates, medium security inmates and maximum security inmates. I have worked in a sexual offender, sexual predator prison. I've worked with death row inmates and also the worst of the worst the Special Needs inmates. This book is just a small portion of the encounters I have had. The reason I no longer work for the department began with a letter I sent to the St. Louis Post Dispatch. I've never been able to keep my opinions to myself especially in the face of bullshit. I didn't think it was necessary to have cowboys run roughshod over the system just because it had always been so. Not only did I speak my mind but I busted some balls in the process. My transfer from Potosi to Farmington was done under protest. Farmington Correctional Center is a dump. It was originally the oldest insane asylum west of the Mississippi I was told. Some of the buildings date back to the civil war era. The newer flat roof buildings leaked like sives. Mold grew in abundance. It was this mold that poisoned my system and forced me to leave the prison system. Let me begin with the letter I sent to the St. Louis Post Dispatch.

Date: 06-29-00

To: Editor, St. Louis Post Dispatch

From: Richard K. Minard

Subject: Death Penalty

I must respond to Robert V. Pambianco's column on the death penalty. I worked at Potosi Correctional Center from July 1995 until July 1999. My wife and I both have degrees in Criminology and Criminal Justice. During the summer of 1995 my wife was given an assignment, for college credit, to interview jurors and their decisions in capital cases. I was fortunate enough to accompany my wife on this assignment. The assignment was to interview jurors that were involved in cases where the death penalty was sought. Some juries decided on death and others chose life without. The amazing thing that I found was the ability of some jurors to browbeat others into decisions that involved life and death. In one case the jury was deadlocked and the deciding factor had to do with the health problems of a relative. They voted against just to get home and take care of an ailing relative. It was the easiest way. The next statement from the individual was, if the relative was not sick the vote may have gone the other way. I am not one to support blue ribbon juries but when the issue is life and death it seems more can be done. I have had the opportunity to work executions. I have been with the victims and I have been with the relatives of the condemned. I have had the unique experience to listen to all sides. I have worked with inmates both capital punishment and life without parole. When I first started working in corrections I was a firm believer in capital punishment. Now I am not. For Robert V. Pambianco to state that "death sentences are reserved for a tiny handful of the worst murders, involving a particularly high degree of violence and cruelty" is not knowing the facts. For every death penalty inmate there are other inmates that have been given life without parole for similar crimes. To state that the death penalty is reserved for particularly heinous or brutal crimes is false. In one case three individuals were involved in a murder. All three were equally guilty. One turned states evidence and got a parolable sentence. The other pled guilty and got parolable life. The other pled not guilty and got the death penalty. Since he pushed the state to a jury trial the prosecutor went for death. And got it. This happens all the time. If you plead to a heinous crime you may get life without. If you don't plead and force a jury trial the prosecutor goes for death. This is wrong. Another argument for the death penalty is that death penalty inmates are somehow more of a threat to society and particularly to corrections staff. Again WRONG. Capital Punishment inmates are no more a threat to corrections staff than those inmates that have life without parole. Why would they be. Another argument for the death penalty is deterrence. The only deterrent effect the death penalty has on criminals is on the inmate being executed. The death penalty exists for one reason only. Revenge. For societies pound of flesh. When we are hurt by these animals we want to hurt back. Let us be honest about it. If revenge is truly what we seek, and it is, then there is no greater punishment than life without parole. Think about it. For the rest of your life you live in what I call the shit soup. No matter how you try you cannot escape the others. You don't want to get involved in others pain but you cant escape it. You don't want to be involved in criminal activity. To do so will get you in trouble. But if someone stronger says you do. Then you do. Television is a curse.

Although it helps pass the time it also reminds you of what you will never have or experience ever again. You would think that to live like this would cause most people to commit suicide. Some do. Some adjust. But most have such a fear of the unknown (hell) that to live in prison until the last moment is all they can do.

Richard K. Minard

WITNESS TO TRAGEDY

"Lets rock n roll" with these words, his last, Andrew Six was led to his death. The execution room itself is nondescript. The walls are concrete block painted glossy white. The gurney itself sits in the center of the room covered in a white sheet. There is a gray steel cabinet that sets in the corner and contains additional bedding just in case.

An hour earlier I was in the execution room inspecting it. I was looking for anything that could be used as a weapon or a tool for suicide. Andy would die on our terms not his and he wasn't taking anyone with him. With the room secure I could move to my next step in the execution process.

When a capital punishment inmate gets his "date" he is placed in administrative segregation. Administrative segregation or Ad-seg is "the hole". There his property and movement are strictly limited so he doesn't cheat the state or find a traveling companion.

At Potosi Correctional Center death row inmates are referred to as capital punishment inmates. There is no death row. Those facing the ultimate punishment are placed in population right beside your run of the mill killer that got life without parole. Executions are scheduled for Tuesday at midnight. The inmate is taken out of the hole the Sunday before and is placed in the holding cell next to the execution chamber. He does not leave this cell for any reason until he is led to his death.

My primary responsibility during the execution process begins early Tuesday the day of the execution. No one from the "outside" is allowed to move unescorted in the prison. My job is to escort the people that choose to visit the condemned one last time. This is almost exclusively family members but occasionally there will be a religious advisor or an attorney. Rarely an attorney. These visits end at 7:00 p.m. The condemned then gets his last meal. The last meal is always interesting to us. I'm not sure why. It is usually no more than a two-liter bottle of Pepsi, fried shrimp or steak, and French fries. Sometimes they ask for ice cream. Nothing elaborate. The last meal is perfunctory. They don't taste it.

At ten o'clock the witnesses begin to arrive. There are three groups of witnesses. Those that witness for the state, those that witness for the victim and those that witness for the condemned. I have had the opportunity to escort at one time or another each group but my primary responsibility was the victims witnesses. It was during this escort detail that I met Mrs. Allen one of Andy's victims.

The first time I saw Andy Six he was locked up in ad-seg. Nothing about him stood out. Short, curly hair, gray pallor, this not only describes Andy but a pretty good portion of the inmate population. Andy was locked up for his own protection. He had, yet again, asked for protective custody due to threats of death against him. This revolving door in and out of ad-seg for protective custody never ends for someone like Andy. His crime was such that he was placed at the bottom of the food chain in prison. Not only a baby raper but also a baby killer and to top it all off the little girl was handicapped. He wasn't tough just stupid. Without a rep to carry him in general population anyone could make their bones by, if not kicking his ass, at least threatening to kill him and so it went for Andy. All he could do is try to stay alive until the state decided to kill him. That threat would be carried out.

I always wonder how men like Andy end up where they do. What is it in their biology that allows them to kill. I would also ask that same question of their psyches but its the same thing. Psychology is no more than biology that we have yet to understand. The other factor and one we can look at is societal. Did something happen to Andy that fueled an inner rage that allowed him to kill. In all of my conversations with him he could not find an answer. When pressed he would blame drugs. Most killers do. If there was a societal influence I would have to say it was his uncle Donald Petary. His partner in this crime. When Andy and I would talk you could tell how much he hated his uncle. It was palpable. The story inside was that Andy did the killing while Don watched and masturbated. A real piece of work. Both would die for this crime.

At 9:50 p.m. on August 20 1997 Mrs. Janet Allen arrived at Potosi Correctional Center. She was wearing a light blue dress. It would be my responsibility to make sure her visit to Potosi would be as comfortable and uneventful as possible. The last thing we need during an execution is problems. I would stick to her like glue from the time she came onto the parking lot until she left the same way she came.

The first time I laid eyes on her I could sense her anxiety. She had driven clear across the state. A drive of several hours. I walked up to her car to introduce myself and noticed that she was praying. I waited a respectful few moments until I thought she was done and approached her car so she would have to acknowledge my presence. During the evening of an execution the institution is on maximum alert. Even the Director has to be officially recognized. Standing on the parking lot for an extended period of time makes the Emergency Squad nervous. I new I only had a very short period of time to get her inside before the E-squad surrounded her car. This she did not need. I introduced myself and the moment she popped her door latch I grabbed the door opened it and started asking her about her drive. I had to get her inside as soon as possible. You have to understand there are three groups of witnesses and none of them can meet while at the institution. That could be a disaster.

There is always a certain feeling you get when you meet people. It is partly instinctual. Working in prison helps you to hone this ability. It is magnified. Fear on the inside is different than fear on the outside. Hate, anger, and fear is the stock in trade in prison. On the outside a child gets lost in a store and is crying. If you look upon this scene you sense the fear in this child. On the inside a small, weak inmate is continually raped and beaten. This is where the magnification comes in. I sensed a great strength in Mrs. Allen as we walked into the prison. Her blue dress, that would probably be described as matronly, covered her from the ankles to the neck. It was only when she turned a certain way that you could see the scar. The scar on her neck was wide and a bit jagged. Whoever did this had put a lot of force behind it. They meant to kill. But Mrs. Allen was not going to give up the ghost. I've always had a great deal of respect for people that walk through hell and come out strong. This is the sense I got when I met Mrs. Allen

From ten o'clock until midnight on the night of an execution the minutes seem like hours. Other than last minute preparations and making sure everybody is comfortable there is a lot of down time. Things get quiet. People are nervous. The closer it comes to the moment of execution the more nervous and quiet people become. Very little chit chat. Not even nervous humor. Almost to a person we take our work seriously. Deadly serious it is. The night Mrs. Allen had the unfortunate experience of being with us it was not this way.

As soon as I got Mrs. Allen settled in I went to get her some water. As I was drawing the water from the water cooler I heard singing coming from the area I'd just left. It was a gospel hymn. It broke the silence like a thunderclap. I horridly went back to my area to see what was going on and when I rounded the corner sure enough Mrs. Allen was singing. She pleasantly finished her song, looked at me, held her hand out for the water and said, "they killed my daughter, they tried to kill me but they will not kill my spirit. God gives me strength when I'm singing."

Being on the buckle in the bible belt most everyone understood what she meant. Whatever gets you through it I say. She continued singing and was joined by some that knew the verses. I asked that they just keep it low and they respectfully complied.

Things got quiet again when she showed me the scar on her neck. This I was not expecting. She told me that it helps to talk about the murder especially now that Andy was only minutes away from meeting his maker. She asked if Andy had found God and I told her I thought he had. This was a lie. Andy had no more found God than I'd won the lottery. Since Andy had gotten locked up he hated everything and everybody. I guess he figured it was too late to repent.

The day it happened was like any other. In rural America since there are few cotillions to attend or country club functions to take your mind off of life you live. You work, you play, you fret. You live. Mr. Allen had had heart problems for some time. It got to the point that they needed money for him and the only way to get it was to sell the pick-up. They placed an ad in the paper and told some friends that the truck was for sale. It was this innocent act that brought Andrew Six and Donald Petary into their lives and their lives would be horribly and permanently altered.

Kathy Allen was twelve years old. The description everyone uses when speaking about her is that she was sweet. A sweet little girl. She had had more than her share of struggles growing up. She was handicapped. She went to a special school for handicapped children. She did what all kids do but with some struggle. She loved and obeyed her parents. She loved God and prayed. She sometimes got on the nerves of her sister especially at this time of year. This time of year is magical for some handicapped kids and Kathy was no exception. She had been looking forward to the Special Olympics for some time. She was so excited about them that that was all she talked about.
She was going to be entered this year.

Donald Petary and Andrew Six had been hanging out and drinking and drugging for several days. Donald wanted a pickup truck. Now, you have to understand how a criminal thinks. When a criminal wants something in their mind they already own it. It is just a matter of time and logistics until they actually posses it. This covers everything from murder to stealing. There is no such thing as deterrence. A criminal mind does not entertain the thought of getting caught. Donald was just this type of criminal. Although Andy's record was not as bad if he had gotten caught for every criminal act he did he would have been in prison. A criminal does not get caught the first time they commit a crime. Some commit crimes all their lives and never get caught. These are the exceptions. If you push it too long though, eventually you get caught but every time you skate you push a little harder. This was Andy. His uncle Donald had served some time. Nothing serious but he had made his bones and Andy wanted to impress his uncle. A pussy acting the badass. A dangerous combination.

Donald Petary had lived in the same area as the Allen's some years before and knew of them. This and his desire for a pickup truck and Andy's desire for rape is what brought them to the Allen's house at around ten o'clock on the evening of April 11. Although it was an odd time for someone to test drive a truck the Allen's were trusting and desperate to sell. Donald explained to Mr. Allen that they would leave their station wagon there. With this he felt assured that it was O.K. Donald and Andy were gone until midnight. Mr. Allen felt so secure that after they were gone for a while he got tired and went to bed.

The plan was to rob the Allen's, take the pickup and kidnap and rape the daughters. Although Andy would have been O.K. with this Donald wasn't. Donald did not want to go back to prison. He knew what was going to be necessary in order to not go back. Donald was not a killer but none are until they do. Andy was eager to make his bones so he could gain the respect of his uncle. They pulled into the driveway of the Allen's anticipating the next step in the plan. It was midnight now and quiet when they stepped out of the truck.

Andy's heart was racing when he stepped out of the truck. The thought of what was about to happen made him more horney than he had ever been in his life. Although rape is about power it is also about sex. Donald and Andy approached the trailer each with his own agenda. Donald entered first with Andy right behind him. Donald looked at Mrs. Allen and demanded the title to the truck. With this Mrs. Allen knew something was terribly wrong. Andy looked hard at the girls and barked at them to get dressed. The noise brought Mr. Allen out of the bedroom. As soon as Donald saw him he pulled out a large knife and Andy pulled out his pocket knife. Pointing to Mr. Allen with the knife Donald told him to sit down. They had brought with them some duct tape for this very reason. Andy taped Mr. Allen to the chair. The entire time Mr. Allen was asking them to leave them alone and that they could have anything they wanted. Andy knew what he wanted. With the girls dressed Donald was leading a procession out to the car. He grabbed Kathy by the arm, to lead them, Christine followed and Andy brought up the rear with his knife pointed at Mrs. Allen's neck. As they were leaving Mr. Allen freed himself and with all the strength he could muster he attacked. Donald bolted for the station wagon dragging Kathy with him. Christine ran into the darkness fleeing for her life. Andy reacted out of fear and terror. Without a conscience thought he pressed the knife blade against Mrs. Allen's throat and pulled. He immediately felt the heat from the wound and as Mrs. Allen placed her hand to her throat he released her and she fled. Andy bolted for the station wagon.

Kathy was now all alone in the station wagon with Andy and Donald. The scene she had just witnessed left her numb. All she could say over and over again was "don't hurt me, please and momma". Donald wanted quiet. He told Andy to "shut that bitch up". Andy smiled at the thought of the many ways to shut her up. What he did instead was to unbutton the girls pants, pull her zipper down and put his hand inside of her panties. He worked his fingers over her soft pubic hair, felt for the soft inner flesh then violently shoved two fingers in side of her as brutally as he could. She gave an involuntary gasp as the pain seized her. "He said shut up bitch didn't you hear him". With this he pulled his hand out of her jeans and smelled his fingers. "This bitch aint no virgin there aint no blood". Donald was in his own world thinking about their next move.

Donald knew that they were screwed. Andy was too stupid and concerned about rape to care. To Donald Kathy was baggage. To Andy she was going to be a part of his twisted fantasies. They crossed into a rural area of Missouri on a back highway and pulled over. Donald made the decision to get rid of Kathy. Andy wanted to keep her. Donald knew that, considering their situation, that it would be impossible. Andy was too stupid to know any better.

It is impossible to know how Kathy was feeling at the time or what she was thinking. Fear perhaps but beyond that. Alone. There is a feeling that most of us will never experience. True aloneness.

If the stories on the inside are true Andy did the killing. A single stab wound. Mrs. Allen told me that the wound was not in and of itself fatal but she bled to death. Alone, hurt and scared. A combination of emotions that I pray I never experience. This is why the death penalty is controversial. Some people truly deserve to die for their brutality. Andy was one of them.

When the clock struck 11:50 p.m. we were in position to bring the witnesses to the execution chamber. I always ask the person I'm escorting if they are really O.K. with viewing the execution. Mrs. Allen was no exception. Viewing the execution of Andy was necessary for her. As we walked down to the execution chamber I could hear Mrs. Allen mumbling a hymn. We took our seats on the platform and waited. The wait is, at times, almost unbearable. Every minute seems to go on forever. What goes on inside the execution chamber cannot be seen until the curtains are opened. Communication is done by radio. When the word is given that all is in place the curtains are opened. You wait what seems like a very long time just staring at a set of curtains. When the curtains open the scene is surreal. The room is incredibly bright, stark white walls and there lays Andy on the gurney looking no different than when I saw him and spoke with him just hours before. The official with the audio headset starts to announce the beginning of the end. Mrs. Allen is visibly nervous and praying under her breath. The official announces that the first drug is being administered. Mrs. Allen places her hand on my arm and squeezes gently. Andy involuntarily coughs lightly and raises his chest and his chest falls and he closes his eyes. The official announces that the second drug is being administered. Mrs. Allen again squeezes my arm gently. I pat the top of her hand and look at her and she is transfixed by what she sees. The official announces that the third drug is being administered. I look at Andy and he looks like he is sleeping. The official announces that the physician has pronounced Andy deceased. Mrs. Allen starts to sing again loud this time. The curtains close and we begin the escort to the press area.

Most victim witnesses do not speak with the press afterwards. Mrs. Allen wanted to. Those that support the death penalty must justify its necessity. Christians, by and large, use the bible. Eye for an eye and all that. Mrs. Allen answered the questions in typical fashion. This tragedy has visited too many people, destroyed too many lives. Is justified by the bible and hopes it brings closure. All true.

As I escorted Mrs. Allen back to her car she said she hoped Andy let God come into his heart. If he truly did then he would be in heaven. He didn't so he must be in hell. I think that's good for Kathy.

JOE THE PIMP

Rape in prison is a given. If you take young males age 17 to 35 which is the peak libido period and remove all females that they can have sex with what is a guy to do. Masturbation gets old. Homosexuals are sometimes willing partners. But what happens mostly is rape. For as many proclivities that exist on the outside so it goes on the inside. From straight? sex to "the freaks." Much of the rape is through manipulation. Intimidation, drug use, favors and protection. Manipulation takes the form of ; "blood on my knife or shit on my dick you decide" or "either I can fuck you or all of them will fuck you" or "if you owe you blow" the owe is usually for drugs. Heroin being the drug of choice for the "pimps."

Joe the pimp is one of the most prolific pimps I met at Potosi Correctional Center. His reputation preceded him. Before he came into my office I was warned about his "charming" personality. I was told he was the master of "smile in your face fuck you in the ass". He was. He was a student of the Dale Carnegie school of bullshit. Joe had been down for a long time. He killed a guy while in prison and got life. The reason I called him into my office was that an officer saw him getting friendly with a new, young man of Asian descent.

A missing person report in an upscale part of St. Louis county turned into a homicide when the body of a young man was found partially buried near a school. The investigation revealed a love triangle of sorts. The young mans best friend was dating a girl that the young man liked. Unable or unwilling to compete with his friend he shot him dead.

His parents were both doctors so in prison the pimps were putting on their best to "befriend" him. Doctors as parents meant a consistent source of funds for the young man and the pimp that would put him in his stable.

Joe got him and what a prize he was. Joe convinced him that he needed protection and Joe was just the benevolent person to give it. Joe didn't have to waste good heroin on him. Heroin is used for the hard cases. The kid was scared, he would do anything Joe told him to. And he did.

I had moved out of that unit and was working in the S.N.U. when I heard about an incident that occurred between Joe and the young man. Joe manipulated some idiot staff member into putting he and the young man in a cell together. Joe convinced the young man's parents that he was their sons protector and they were grateful. Joe went to visits with the young man when his parents came to see him. In the visiting room the visitor can bring in up to $ 25.00 in change for the snacks and smokes machines. The young man received a visit from his parents and Joe naturally went also.

During the visit Joe kept pushing the young man to eat and drink. This would have been odd because Joe would have used most of the money for himself. As soon as the visit was over the young man and Joe went back to their housing unit. Shortly thereafter there was an incident in a cell in their unit and a call went out that there was an assault in progress. When the officers arrived they found the young man naked on the floor beat to shit and lying in his own vomit. The vomit was a combination of the snacks he had just consumed in the visiting room and semen.

It turned out that the inmate that assaulted the young man had been badgering Joe to get a blow job from the young man. Joe kept putting him off because he already owed Joe. On the promise that he would pay up Joe said yes. The whole situation was set up. Joe wanted the guy off his back. Joe knew that the young man gagged and sometimes vomited when Joe demanded that he swallow. Joe set up the blow job for after the visit. Joe so generously allowed the young man to fill his stomach with snacks and sodas. As the young man and his aggressor were led away in cuffs to the hole Joe was seen on the top walk laughing with the other pimps.

RELEASES

An inmates' last few months are critical if they are to ever have a chance at a normal life on the outside. At Potosi there are so few releases that pre-release preparations are ignored. This is a critical mistake. Because there are so few releases the resources exist to do it right. The idea of helping an inmate transition into society is foreign to most staff. Help may equate with empathy. They are not empathetic.

The worst example of this was a release from the infirmary to the street. Bill was crazy. He was a self mutilator that constantly threatened suicide. He made it to Potosi by way of write ups at a lower level institution. Since he was crazy he couldn't follow orders. Not following orders gets you write ups. Too many write ups and you end up in maximum security. That's one reason why SNU exists but more on that later.

Bill was scheduled to be released to the Salvation Army Harbor Lights Mission. The only place he could go since he had no where else to go. A couple of months prior to Bills release another inmate was released to Salvation Army at Kansas City. He never showed up. Somewhere between Potosi and Kansas City he disappeared. The Salvation Army made an inquiry but what can you do. If an inmate is released after serving his sentence he's free to go where he pleases even if he is crazy and violent with, quite possibly, a strong libido. The inquiry made the department nervous. They didn't want the press to report that an inmate released from Potosi just hopped off the bus and killed or raped someone. Bill was scheduled for a Saturday release. The week before, he was admitted to the infirmary for a suicide attempt or threat. On Friday night when the evening meal was served (brown bag only for suicidal inmates) he asked the inmate porter if he would like to trade a sandwich for fruit. The porter said O.K. because he didn't like fruit but could use an extra sandwich. He asked the officer if it was O.K. and he said sure. The officer opened the food port to Bills cell and the trade was made. The porter sat down to eat and took a big bite of his sandwich. He immediately spit it out and screamed "what the fuck is this". Bill had taken a shit, took the meat off of his sandwich and ate it and replaced it with shit, a shit sandwich. The porter threw up the officer gagged and Bill just laughed and laughed. The next morning, Saturday, Bill was placed in handcuffs and leg irons, driven to Harbor Lights, taken to the door where the cuffs and irons were removed and told to go inside. He did.

No matter what an inmates status is on the inside when the times up it is up. When an inmate finishes his sentence he is released. Many inmates "max out" their sentences and then some. If you refuse to follow orders or commit crimes on the inside you lose your good time date. Rick was one of these. If you get a sentence of 2–10 yrs. the court is telling you that if you get your shit together you could be home soon. If not see, ya' next decade idiot. Rick was the latter. Rick was small and young when he came to prison. When he arrived at Jefferson City Correctional Center it had been dubbed the bloodiest prison in the U.S. because of all the stabbings. The Aryan Brotherhood had recently been formed and the racial tension was at an all time high. The prison itself was ancient. The oldest prison west of the Mississippi. Maintenance tunnels, blind corners and the sheer extensiveness of the prison allowed the inmates to pretty much run the place. And they did. Rick came in on a small bit (sentence). He was quickly punk'd (raped and turned out) by the blacks. As far as the Aryans were concerned he was dead to them so he got no protection. Young, small and on his own he had to do what he was told by his pimp. Not only does a punk bitch have to put out to anyone the pimp tells him to he also has to do anything the pimp tells him to. This means holding all of the pimps contraband. Drugs, shanks (knives) anything. About the only thing a pimp has to do himself is maintain his rep. (reputation). If someone disrespects the pimp the pimp has to handle it. If a pimp allows one of his bitches to even the score he losses all respect and pretty soon his stable is challenged and lost. A pimp only exists on his reputation. Every inmate benefits by this situation if they are so inclined. The Aryans, whites, also benefit. They like blow jobs and anal sex also.

Through stupidity and manipulation Rick lost his good time date. By the time he was ready for release he was an old punk. He had tired of the game years before. At some point he told his pimp fuck you, probably took a beating, and was on his own. Over the years he developed a talent as a tattoo artist. His artwork was very good and he could put together a tattoo gun with a minimum of equipment. This usually consists of a battery, the motor out of a cassette player, an ink pen and a small piece of guitar string. His reputation as a top tattoo artist spread and soon his was in high demand. He had so many tattoo "guns" taken from him that the number of write ups he received got him rolled to Potosi. He only had four months left on his sentence when he got to Potosi. Everyone rolled from one prison to another on violations goes to the hole. Usually within seven to ten days they are seen by a committee to determine their best placement. Rick was pissed off when he got rolled. No one wants to leave "home" and it was because of his attitude that he stayed in ad-seg. Since he was going to 12-12 (finish your sentence with no parole afterward) in four months there was no sense letting him out to set up shop.

He was at Potosi only a few days when his mom called me. She explained to me that she had a job all lined up for Rick at a tattoo shop and that his artwork was being shown everywhere. She railed to me about how the department screwed her "baby" and was continuing to do so by keeping him in ad-seg. She also thanked me for the certificates of recognition he received from the department for his outstanding achievements in art and that his artwork would hang at the gallery in Jefferson City. Rick could spin a yarn. The only recognition Rick received from his art in prison got him sent to the hole. There is no gallery. Rick hand made the certificates and sent them to his mom. We found one in his property. Very well done. Rick did his time in ad-seg with a minimum of problems. After all ad-seg was a second home to him. He went straight from the hole to the bus. No release preparation no one to greet him when he got out. The next time Rick came to my attention was when I was reading the newspaper. There was a story about a double murder in a rural Missouri town. As I read the story I recognized that the murderer was Rick. It seemed that Rick had hooked up with a couple of guys from his old days in prison. Rick had borrowed his moms gun just to be bad. He and his two buddies went out drinking and they picked up two women. They went back to one of his buddies house. When the talk turned to sex the truth came out that Rick was a punk in prison. This is something Rick wanted no one to know or speak about. The humiliation was just too great. The women left and Rick waited until his two "friends" passed out. He shot them each in the head as they slept.

DRUG SMUGGLING

There are more drugs in prison than out on the street. I've heard this said many times and it may be true. The populations of prisons are small so it doesn't take much dope to saturate the place. Drugs are used to get high of course but they are truly used for manipulation. Pimps use them to incur debts and also to deaden the pain of rape.

But how do drugs get in prison. There are many ways but there are two in particular. One is through the visiting room and the other is through staff bringing them in. As long as there are contact visit's the visitors will bring in drugs. Some prisons go so far as to allow food visits. At Potosi the only food visits that were allowed were in the honor houses and that food had to come from an approved vendor. The inmate would order say a pizza or chicken dinner from one of the restaurants in town. This would be handled through the recreation department and would be delivered on visiting day. They had these a couple of times per year. At Farmington they had food visits all the time. People were allowed to bring in homemade food as well as food provided by a vendor. Even though they checked the food the drugs were still smuggled in. Very tiny condoms filled with heroin about the size of a bean mixed in with ham and beans. Aluminum foil on the bottom of a cake held sheets of LSD. I even heard of one person that mixed in very strong brown pot in a small chocolate cake. The inmate went back to his cell threw up the cake on some paper, dried the paper and then had a pretty good stash of pot. Sounds sick but if they are desperate to get high they can be creative. Women put drugs in their vaginas then remove them in the restroom. The trustees come by and empty the waste can. Every loud incident that focuses the officers attention to one area allows others to pass their dope. All choreographed of course.

The inmates wives, girlfriends, parents, grandparents, kids, brothers, sisters, cousins you name it will swarm the visiting room on one particular day. Ten or more inmates operate a ring to smuggle in drugs. They will do whatever it takes to bring the dope in. The tighter the security the more elaborate the smuggling operation. They know that some may be found but not all of it. It's just like on the street. The cartels know some will be found that's just a part of doing business.

The other way drugs find there way into prison is through staff. At Potosi this was a rarity. The reason is that it is in a rural setting. Although Potosi is a poor area and you would think that the money made off of drugs would be tempting the closeness of the people stops it. If you got caught the humiliation to you and your family would be devastating. The chances of getting caught out ways the risk for most people.

The money factor though is not the only reason staff take the chance. Although the situation is rare it does happen through manipulation. A trustee was cleaning the recreation area one morning as a part of his normal duties. He had an early visit so he asked his supervisor, an officer, if he could come in early so he could get off early to clean up for his visit. His supervisor O. K.'d the situation and he started an hour early. At the back of the gym there is a

small room where they hand out equipment. This is where he normally started his work. As he approached the room he heard some
noises. He walked in quietly and found two officers having sex.
Both were married and the male officers wife worked at the prison.
Busted. Had the inmate reported what he saw there would have to
be an investigation. The trustee told a few friends and pretty soon
they had him bringing in drugs. The officer couldn't stand the
thought of his wife even suspecting he was cheating but in the end
he got caught not only for infidelity but for drug smuggling.
Another case of manipulation is the smooth tongued devil. Most
inmates practice manipulation to a high art form. Since they lack
the conscience necessary to feel bad about what they say and do they
become masters. Women staff in prison are their chosen quarry. It is
critical that in prison you do not self disclose. The more they know
about you the more ammunition you give them. And hunt you they
will. A female staff member had been going through an ugly
divorce. She was suffering from depression. Her situation had been
going on for years. After the divorce she lost some weight and
started looking better. She worked closely with an inmate clerk and
confided in him at times. He was a good looking guy and knew all
the right words. He enjoyed getting high and gambling. He also
hated prison and would do anything to get out. He started pushing
all of the right buttons. He would compliment her on how good she
looked and then apologize for getting too personal. This type of
exchange went on for a while and pretty soon the apologies stopped.
She's flattered. One day he shows up at work with a black eye. She
asked what happened and he is tight lipped. She pries it out of him
that he has a large gambling debt. Now, she knows he can't/won't
go to staff and report it. An inmate is pretty much on his own with

debts unless he wants to live in protective custody. By this time she is in love and demands that she help him. He tells her that if he had some pot to give the dude he would call it square. She is not into drugs but he assures her that all she has to do is meet a friend of his and he will give her the drugs. Only on rare occasions, randomly, do they search staff. She brings in the drugs and everything is cool. Now she is hooked. All she had to do is bring it in one time and he's got her. Most pot that comes into prison is in small quantities. One sixteenth ounce, maybe one eighth ounce. He had her bringing in ounces. This quantity of dope does not go unnoticed in prison. He's still an inmate and egotistical. He's also setting her up for the big score. Not drugs but a gun. He figures if she can smuggle in a gun he can take a hostage and walk on out. Through what seemed to be mere coincidence one morning the area that she worked in was being searched. The officers got a tip on where there might be some metal that had been missing. She brought in some pot and since the prison was locked down because of the search the inmate could not come by and pick it up. During the search of her area the pot was found. Through an intensive investigation everything was revealed including the plan for the gun. The real sad part was that her son also worked at the prison as an officer.

ESCAPE

The Religious Freedom Reformation Act passed in 1993 allowed for more types of religions to be practiced in prisons. Not only could they practice but the states had to provide similar resources for all religions. No religion could be denied access to the chapel. Christians would use the chapel for services and then the witches could use the same chapel for WICCA services. Spiritual leaders gained access to the prison who would have been denied before the act. Ex cons that were now ministers could gain access. As religious advisers they were treated with special care. Searches were perfunctory at best. This allowed for much dope to be smuggled in. Certain ceremonies were conducted in private. This allowed for the inmates to plan any number of illegal activities.

At Potosi the most controversial of all of the adjustments was the sweat lodge. There were a half dozen or so Native Americans at the prison. Their religious ceremonies could not be conducted in a church. They had to have a sweat lodge. A sweat lodge is used to sweat. This means that they need fire. This means that they needed wood. Not only that but they had to split the wood themselves. This meant they needed an ax. At Potosi any metal in the hands of inmates is forbidden or extremely closely monitored. Only the most trustworthy inmates gets to use metal tools and they are closely monitored. Now the state said that just because you are a Native American you can have access to a chopping ax. Thoughts of Jack

Nicholson in The Shining come to mind. If there is one group of inmates in the Missouri prison system that tries above all others to escape it is the Native Americans.

It wasn't long before there was an incident. The prison had been placed on immediate lockdown because of a stabbing. This means that every inmate must immediately return to his cell. The inmates at the sweat lodge were notified to return to their cells. One inmate refused. He was a pain in the ass inmate that was always in trouble. White man this. White man that. Typical bullshit. A code was called to clear the sweat lodge area and he grabbed the ax. Now directly above the sweat lodge about eighty feet was the tower. In the tower was an officer armed with an M-16. The officers surrounded the sweat lodge and told him to drop the ax. He refused. They tried to talk him out of his situation but he told them to get fucked. They would not interrupt his sweat. One officer got on the radio to the tower and within earshot of the inmate told the tower guard to put the crosshairs on the inmates chest. He was going in to get the ax. He told the officer that if he looked like he was going to swing to take him out. The officer approached the inmate and he just about shit. He dropped the ax immediately and fell face down on the ground. The officer was reprimanded for stupidity and the tower guard was replaced.

The sweat lodge was used to plan the greatest escape attempt at Potosi. A tunneling operation that still blows my mind when I think about it. The way it was discovered was that an inmate in the minimum security unit was going through the trash. All trash cans have trash bags placed in them that are marked with there location. All trash coming from the within the security envelop is given a cursory check. During one of these searches they found a milk carton with dirt and rock in it. At first they didn't know what they had. An inmate in the minimum security unit that had worked in the area said it was sub dirt. Dirt that was disturbed when you level an area. Now they suspected they had a tunnel. An immediate lockdown was called. Every inch of every cell and every area within the security envelop was searched. The cell that it was found in had been searched twice. The cover of the hole was painted and blended in perfectly. It sat solid so if it was walked on you couldn't tell. What amazed me was that the concrete floor was eight inches thick of dense concrete with two inch rebar spaced about six inches apart. They chipped through the concrete using a busted screwdriver and half of a ten pound dumbbell. Only the inmates involved knew how they cut the rebar and they weren't talking. The tunnel itself was also amazing. The terrain around that area is rock. They kept encountering rock and they just chipped through it. At first the tunnel went in one direction. At some point they abandoned this direction and started in a new direction. When the tunnel was found it was determined that if they had kept going in the original direction they would have made it outside the fence. It was also determined that the period of time it took to dig the tunnel was about the same period of time that the sweat lodge had been functional. RFRA gave them a place to plan their escape.

BIG B. S.

He embodied the description big bellied sheriff. Over six feet tall and pushing three hundred plus pounds. His normal weight should have been no more than one eighty. A gut that stretched his shirts to bursting. He had a southern accent that wasn't slow but twangy. He sounded like an out of tune violin. He never went anywhere without his cheek full of chew. Skoal was the preferred brand of most tobacco chewers. As was his. He always carried a coffee cup with him in order to have a receptacle for his spit. You would think he was addicted to coffee but one look in the cup showed otherwise. A disgusting habit turned into an addiction. One look at him on most days and you could tell some of what he had had for lunch. Since his gut was so big he was forced to sit further away from the table than his coordination could handle. This usually meant a bit of his meal ended up on his shirt. On occasion, when the chief of security was out of the prison, he would be in charge. One day the word came down from the state capital that tobacco was not permitted in almost every area of the prison. Inmates could smoke in their cells or you could smoke outside but that was it. This included chewing tobacco. The telltale cup would have to go but he was not going to give up his chew. A dilemma ensued. What to do with the spit. His solution was to spit behind open doorways. When his mouth filled with spit he would find an open door, pull it away from the wall and spit on the backside of it. This solved his problem. His solutions to problems were always along these lines. One day a parcel delivery driver inadvertently left a fairly large box by the front entrance door. A call was made to the security offices to find out what should be done with it. Don't touch it was the reply that came back. Inquiries were made. Where did it come from? No one knew. How long had it been there? Again no one could answer. The contents were a mystery. A decision was made to evacuate the area just in case the box posed a hazard. By now everyone in the prison knew about the situation. My god were we under attack by forces unknown bent on our destruction. Was this some sort of escape attempt. The incoming phone lines were monitored just in case. When the head security officer on duty heard of the situation he responded immediately. It had taken him a few minutes to arrive on the scene. He assessed the situation and determined that it may in fact be a bomb. But how to tell for sure. Would he contact the Missouri state highway patrol bomb squad? Well, if he did that and it wasn't a bomb he would be embarrassed and he didn't like that. His solution was simple. He stood about forty feet back from the box and ran toward it as fast as his legs could propel his three hundred pound self and he kicked the box as hard as he could and kept on running. The last I heard about him he had been arrested a second time for stalking a fellow employee that he had been dating.

FARMINGTON

When I transferred from Potosi I went to Farmington Correctional Center. It had the dubious distinction of being the sex offender prison for the state. It was also medium security. If professionalism was hard to find at Potosi then at Farmington it was non-existent. There was a superintendent in charge of a treatment unit that was a pig. His clothes always looked like he slept in them. He always had stains on his clothes. His hair was always a mess. And he was suppose to set the standard. My apologies to the pigs. There were a few who strove for professionalism but they were overwhelmed. The people directly under him, who were supervisors, held the state record for having more grievances filed against them by their workers than any other group of supervisors. And this was supposed to be a treatment center. No treatment going on there.

The big difference between maximum and medium security is parole. Just about everyone in medium security will be released some day so they are less likely to rock the boat. Because of this, policy and procedure was ignored. In maximum security the policy manual is what runs the show. It's the policy manual that gives the inmates what they have coming. It defines their treatment. At Farmington it was what you could get away with. My reputation proceeded me to Farmington. I was a marked man. I was given a chair. No desk, no office, no assignment, no supervisor no nothing. I had to contact the assistant director in order to get a place to hang my hat. They gave me an assignment looking into some complaints that new inmates were filing on being raped. I interviewed the new inmates and they all told me the same story. All of the inmates that were raped were young, small and white. They pointed out the same inmate as their rapist. I asked the inmate that was doing the assaults about it and he, of course, denied it.

I wrote up the report and stated that if the same evidence were presented in court then he would possibly be convicted. I was told that these are sex offenders ratting on a sex offender. I turned in my report. I was given another assignment.

Eventually I worked my way in to the Reception and Orientation unit. This is where you greet the new fish. Since there was a lot of paperwork involved I was given two inmate clerks to help me. One of the inmates was a big fellow that had been in for twenty years on a murder charge. Meeting him would prove the old saying that it's a small world. His name was Bob. In my late teens I had been kicking around not doing much. I had dropped out of school and would take odd jobs for dope money. A friend of mine Steve, dead now, had a sister who was married to a real asshole. There was only one more person I knew who was a bigger asshole and that was his brother. But they had a roofing company. Steve got me a job with them one summer pouring hot roof. The job sucked. I worked the first week and when Friday came I was told that since the job wasn't finished I wouldn't get paid until the next Friday. The next Friday came and I was expecting two weeks pay. I only got one and was told that I would be paid in full next Friday when the new job was done. On Monday morning when Steve came by to get me I told him to shove the job up his ass. I knew his brother in law was trying to fuck me. Steve worked that week and when Friday came he only got half a weeks pay. Steve also quit. Screwed by his own brother in law. Like I said they were assholes. A couple of weeks later one of the brothers turned up missing. His wife reported it. They found his truck on the parking lot of a strip mall. When they searched the camper they found his body. He was shot once in the head. Steve's family reacted in typical white trash fashion vowing to find and kill the bastard/'s responsible. The cops found out that a large insurance policy had been taken out on the guy only a few weeks prior to his murder. The wife crumbled like dirt and told all. She hired a guy to do the killing and now they were both busted. The years passed and Steve got hit by a truck on the highway. He was drunk.

As I looked at Bob's file the memories started to flood back. As I read I figured out that this was the guy that killed the guy that owed me a weeks pay. I called Bob into my office just to talk. I asked him what he was in for and he reluctantly said for murder. I asked him if he knew a couple of people that I knew he knew. He got nervous and I could tell he was getting very uncomfortable. I then told him the story about how the guy owed me money and that I wasn't sure if he deserved to be killed but he surely was an asshole. Bob and I worked fine together after that.

PROTECTIVE CUSTODY

If an inmate can no longer reside in general population the prison is bound by law to provide that individual with protective custody P.C.. Until very recently that usually meant living in the hole. Twenty three hour a day lock down, no privileges and very little property. Lawsuits filed by inmates have changed that. Now most prisons have protective custody housing units. They receive the same privileges and property as general population inmates also some yard time and open unit movement. In order to qualify for protective custody you have to have enemies in the general population and be able to positively identify them. If the inmate is not willing or able to do this they don't qualify. Many an inmate has been refused protective custody because of their inability to do this.

The way the process works is like this. An inmate is in a fight for example or simply walks up to a staff member and requests protective custody. All other inmates within the immediate area are or should be cleared from that area. The inmate is then secured, cuffed, the yard is or should be locked down and the inmate is taken to the hole. The reason I put should be in the above sentences is because at Potosi this was always done per law but at Farmington it was rarely done. At Farmington policies and laws were meant to be broken. After the inmate is placed in the hole his property from his previous cell is secured and sent to the central property storage area. During this time is when much of his property is stolen. Once the word gets out that he has checked in he is labeled a punk or a bitch. Check ins are just a step above child molesters and baby rapers. A committee then reviews the inmates situation, looks at what a possible investigation, if necessary, may have revealed and then interviews the inmate to find out the particulars. If it has been determined that the inmate does qualify then he is placed on the list and waits for an open bed. There is usually always a list. The inmate stays locked down in the hole until his name comes up. This could take anywhere from a week to a month or longer. If an inmate does not qualify he is given a bed in general population and is ordered to move. Now, inmates are not stupid, if they have a serious situation that they must avoid they will refuse to move, get a write up, and be sentenced to hole time. They will continue to play this game every ten days, the amount of hole time max for refusing to move, until their situation changes or until they name an enemy. Usually they will name someone that they know is an asshole to try to get into protective custody. In this situation the institution will present the inmate with an enemy waiver. An enemy waiver is a form that states basically we are no longer enemies. Both inmates have to sign it or get sent to the hole. The person being accused of being an enemy signs but the inmate trying to get P.C. doesn't so he stays in the hole. It's a game that a lot of inmates play to stay off the yard for one reason or another. There are many reasons why an inmate checks in. A snitch that gets caught, a kid being pressured for sex or has been raped, junkies check in all the time to sober up, debts that can't be paid. An inmate that comes in on a bad case, molester, rapist for example looks to check in as soon as possible but it depends on the inmate.

A young man from St. Louis was sent to Potosi as a C.P.. He got the death penalty. He and some friends were out late one night and went to an old bridge that is shut down that crosses the Mississippi river. On the bridge were two sisters and their male cousin just out having a good time. The sisters frequented the bridge as a place of solace and to write poetry. The two groups ran into each other on the bridge. Why the young men decided to do what they did is why I am a Criminologist. The young men raped and then pushed the girls off of the bridge and into the river. The cousin leapt off of the bridge. Eventually they recovered the bodies of the sisters and the cousin lived. The police were certain that the cousin did it but the young men were caught. Because of his crime and his youth and stature, he was small, it wasn't too long before he was raped. He didn't want to be a punk so he checked in. In a case like this the institution knows what his situation will be and so will grant him protective custody with little formality.

Child molesters are another group that fills the protective custody units. But not always. Dan was a local. He had been arrested in the early 1970's on an assault charge. A pretty bad felony charge but was given probation. In the mid 1980's his son and daughter in law were going through a divorce. He sided with his son and the custody situation involving his granddaughter got ugly. While at work one day the local sheriff showed up and arrested Dan and told him the charges were child molestation. Dan denied it. A nurse at the hospital that examined the little girl said the exam showed physical signs that indicated molestation. Dan was sent to prison as a child molester. He was in his mid 50's about six foot tall and overweight. Nobody ever bothered him. He died of a heart attack at Potosi. What an end. Inmates will use any excuse in order to control another. The idea that child molesters or rapists will fare poorly in prison is part true and part myth. It doesn't really make much difference to most inmates. Of those that have to feel superior they look at molesters as scum. Of those that manipulate and take it's just an excuse to do so.

NIGGER

I had only been at the prison about a couple of months when I heard the word nigger for the first time. My immediate supervisor was talking about buying a car. She had regaled us with a conversation she had had with her husband. She stated that she told her husband that she wanted a Cadillac and his response was that he would never put his butt in a niggers' car. I didn't say anything to my shame and since I didn't I was considered a good ol' boy. Over the next several months I heard the word a couple of more times. I contacted the superintendent in writing and explained to him my concerns. I told him that I thought the term repulsive and if he was concerned about safety he should address this issue. The next day there was a memo issued from his office stating that derogatory remarks were not to be used. Unfortunately, too many department heads didn't know what derogatory meant. I then made it a point to tell my co-workers that I would not tolerate these terms and that if I heard them I would report it. I lost my good ol' boy status. I was also transferred to a different unit.

I had been in my new unit position for a few months when I received a call at home. It was just after midnight and I was told by the officer on call to report to the prison immediately. When I arrived everyone that worked in my unit was there. I had found out that there was a riot in my unit. The uprising had been contained but they were still bringing people out. Our job was to go in and record all of the property that was now being removed from the area. It was also our job to counsel the inmates and try to alleviate the tension. After a staff member is assaulted people tend to get pissed. After a riot it's WWIII. Within about one hundred feet to the entrance of the unit I could smell pepper spray. The closer I got the stronger it was. When I walked into the unit every moist area of my body burned. They had used what is called the Israeli gas gun. This is a high pressure fogger that releases massive amounts of pepper spray over a large area very quickly. I had heard about it but never saw it used. There were only four inmates involved in the mini-riot the rest just had to suck it up. They blocked their doors as best they could to keep the gas out of their cells but it leaked in anyway. Medical personnel was there flushing eyes and doling out aspirin. We worked all night cleaning up the mess, figuratively speaking, and I went home exhausted.

Several weeks later the Director showed up at the prison to pass out awards and give pats on the back to those involved. Conspicuously absent were the two officers that were in the unit when the fight started. Each had been assaulted. What I found out was these two particular officers had no qualms in calling the black inmates nigger to their face. Only a fool doesn't know that this could be suicide. The inmate that threw the first punch was in prison on four counts of second degree murder. He was very young but he was a killer. He told the officer that very evening that if he ever called him nigger again he would kill him. The officer responded by telling him fuck you nigger. The inmate went to the unit phone, ripped the handset from it and started beating the officer with it. It was on.

PATRICK

Patrick was one of the most pathetic characters at Potosi. When I first saw him he was in deep seg and had been for most of his time in prison. He was a young black male with chiseled features. He was not very tall but was built like a bull. He was one of the most muscled inmates I ever saw. He could go from smiling to rage in the snap of a finger. His assaults even on staff were legendary. Jimmy was one of the staff members that found this out first hand. Jimmy was one of the best C.O.'s I ever had the pleasure of working with. He knew how to handle inmates and never took his work personally. He didn't judge the inmates he would say their job is to break the rules and my job is to enforce them. Jimmy would tell of his encounter with Patrick anytime Patrick's name was mentioned.

Patrick had had more movement teams come in on him than almost any other inmate in the system. A movement team is formed anytime an inmate refuses to leave their cell. It's also known as a cell extraction team. There are many reasons why a movement team is put together. If a judge demands that an inmate be present for court and he doesn't want to go that could lead to a movement team being formed. If an inmate refuses to clean his cell until it becomes inhabitable he will be forcefully removed and other inmates will have to clean it. Patrick rarely complied with an order to leave his cell. If an officer went to his door to offer him his daily rec (recreation) he would jump at the chance. This was his chance to work out, stretch his legs and breath outside air. In ad-seg and deep-seg it's 23 in and 1 out. Patrick would take his rec and come back in. If fifteen minutes later he was told he had to leave his cell he would nut-up (refuse). This is how he behaved.

A movement team consists of five officers specially trained for the job. The first man in has the shield to push back the inmate so the other officers can grab him. The shield is plexi-glass about four feet tall. Two men grab arms and two men grab legs. When the inmate is down the shield bearer can set the shield aside to help hold the inmate if necessary. More recently a sixth person has been added to man a video camera. When subdued (stuffed and cuffed) he is removed from the cell. Inmates try all kinds of things to gain an edge. They would flood the cell and/or put lotion or shit or a combination of both or all three on the floor so the officers lose their footing. My first thoughts on why Patrick refused to move was that he enjoyed the sport of it but that idea would change. Jimmy was a part of a movement team that went in on Patrick. He was the man on the shield. As they entered Patrick fought like a bull. When they thought they had his arms and legs Jimmy set the shield aside quickly because they were having trouble holding him. Jimmy jumped on his back to bring him down and as Jimmy would say, "I was tossed like a rag doll". Since they were having such a hard time other officers joined in and eventually Patrick tired. As I worked the segregation units I got to know Patrick better. He asked me one day what it would take to get out of ad-seg and get into a population unit. I told him for starters he would have to stay out of trouble. I checked his file and found out he had hole time extending out about a year. A couple of days later I told him that if he stayed out of trouble for one month I would see what I could do. He succeeded.

When I talked to him again he wanted to be let out. I explained to him that he had about five years of bad time on him and if he was serious about getting out then he would have to give me eleven more months of good time. I told him I would work with him to get him out but if he fucked up just one time then it's over. He said he would do it. Before the eleven months were out I transferred to the SNU. When we were pouring over the files of potential candidates for admittance Patrick's name was on the list. Psychological file material is not readily available to case managers or unit managers. In reading Patrick's file I learned that he suffered from schizophrenia with paranoid delusions. What I had assumed he had done for sport, assaulting staff, was his survival mechanism. Any time he was forced to leave his cell or forced to do anything he thought it was being done to harm him. When we decided to take Patrick into the unit most staff at the institution thought we were nuts. Because of his assaults on staff they were leery that he could change. Patrick was released from ad-seg and brought into the special needs unit. It had been about ten months into the twelve month period of good behavior that I had imposed. He was elated that he got out early. I told him that because he kept his word and stayed out of trouble that not only me but many staff members went to bat for him so that he would have the chance to better himself. The truth was that we had to fight to get him into the unit. In the unit he finally got the medications he needed on a regular basis. He also got some one on one counseling. He was a man-child needing attention. His mother had abandoned him at a very young age. He was moved from foster home to foster home. His mental illness caused him to react violently which is rare. We even got him a job picking up cigarette butts on the yard. One day I was standing out on the yard talking to Jimmy and Patrick was out doing his job Jimmy stated that it was hard to believe Patrick was out and that maybe he just needed a chance. Jimmy is one of the good officers.

JOE

The most infamous inmate I worked with was Joseph Franklin. In the late 1970's he sat outside of a synagogue in St. Louis and as services were letting out he shot a man as he was leaving the synagogue. Joe gained his infamy by shooting, among others, Larry Flynt the publisher and Vernon Jordan the civil rights leader. He was a white separatist/supremacist. The one thing that upset him the most was interracial couples. The reason he shot Larry Flynt was because he published a cartoon of an interracial couple. Now that's crazy.

Joe received the death penalty for the synagogue shooting. He arrived at Potosi the same way all capital punishment inmates do. When an inmate receives the death penalty in Missouri they are taken immediately to Potosi from the county that sentenced them. They do not spend any more time in a county jail than they have to unlike other inmates that may set in a county or city lock up for days or weeks on their way to the prison processing center in Fulton, Missouri. Upon arrival at Potosi Joe was placed in "deep-seg". This is an ad-seg unit that is monitored much more heavily than a normal ad-seg unit. Everything including the shower is in the cell. The capital punishment inmate is placed in a cell that also has a camera in it. We need to make sure that they don't kill themselves and cheat the state. Joe did his week in deep-seg and was then transferred to a regular ad-seg unit. A committee would see him and determine where he would go in general population. Each unit is designed so that an inmate can move up or down the privilege scale. From ad-seg he would go into a very controlled unit with few privileges. This unit is predominately black. The unit with the most privileges and the least restrictive is about 50-50 black and white. An inmate has to work his way to the most privileged unit and it could take about a year. Most never make it. Joe was released from ad-seg and sent to his new home in population. As soon as he saw what his situation was going to be he freaked out. He absolutely refused to cell in the unit. He swore that we were setting him up to be hit. When I talked to him he demanded to be placed in the unit that was 50-50. He asked me why we weren't taking care of him white man to white man. He told me that he thought he would be respected by staff for killing niggers. He was told in jail that Potosi was good for whites. Unfortunately, some of what he said is true but for those in charge. Joe went back to ad-seg. Twenty three hour a day lock down no privileges. This would be his life unless he changed his mind.

ROBERT

I have had the somewhat rare opportunity to speak with and counsel some of the most vile and violent inmates the state of Missouri has to offer. Although I would not want them as neighbors I don't, for the most part, fear them. Robert is the exception. The hate and the rage in him is palpable. He is the type of inmate that does not fear. He fears nothing and nobody. The curious thing about Robert is that he stands about five foot seven and weighs somewhere around one hundred forty five pounds. Not a big guy by any stretch.

In prison the blacks and whites pretty much stay to themselves. Fist fights are usually about grudges and stickings are usually for revenge. I use the term usually because it is not a hard and fast rule. One thing that will piss off the blacks in prison quick is if a white person refers to a black as nigger. That is a huge no no. Robert never gave a shit. He always referred to blacks as niggers. And they never touched him. I asked one of the more level headed inmates why this was. The inmate told me that Robert above all the others was truly evil. He told me about an incident where Robert called a new arrival a nigger. The inmate was rolled to Potosi for write ups at a lower level prison. The inmate could do nothing but kick his ass. He had to save face. Robert was too small to put up much of a fight so he really took a beating. After the fight was over and Robert was released from the infirmary he started staring at the guy. He wouldn't stop. Not for nothing. Seven days a week while he was awake Robert would locate him and stare at him. Non stop. The guy beat his ass again but nothing changed. Robert would not take his eyes off this guy. The inmate complained to me about this and I told Robert to stop. He said he wasn't doing this but if he was and I told him to stop he would tell me "fuck you". Typical Robert response to authority. This continued for weeks until the guy requested protective custody and named Robert as his sworn enemy. The other inmates convinced him that it was the only way unless he wanted a case for murder. Most of the inmates believed he could put curses on people or he was cursed himself.

Robert found his way to prison compliments of his mother. He grew up in small town Missouri and was not made to accomplish anything. Both parents were severe alcoholics and Robert would,at times, tell me about how violent the home was. He thought it was normal to get beat for everything. When Robert was nine his father left for good. He was an only child so it was just him and his mom. Unfortunately for Robert with his dad out of the picture his mom was lonely. She was also too lazy to go out and find another man. Robert would have to suffice. He lost his virginity to his mother and became her lover. Some rural counties have the dubious distinction of family trees that look like more like poles. For the most part this kind of talk is done in jest as a way to rib your county neighbors but for Robert it truly was his life. Oedipus gone wild.

Robert's juvenile and young adult record show many crimes. Mostly petty but some assaults. Incomplete school records that are all too typical for most in prison. His real problem started when his mom finally got up off her lazy ass and found herself a man. Robert had been everything to his mother and vice versa. A young male going through puberty and then young adulthood with a more than willing sex partner this would be heady stuff even if, or especially if, it is your mother. The situation had done psychological damage that is incomprehensible.

Robert's mom came home one day with her new beau. She had to break it to Robert that this man would be his new father and that Robert would have to mind him. She also explained to Robert that the sexual relationship that they were having would have to stop. She told him that it was wrong anyway. Whatever emotion that is more powerful than rage must have seized him. He would not give up his place in his house for anyone. For years he was literally the man of the house and now at age seventeen he was not going to give up his spot. Robert attacked his moms new lover several times. They were constantly fighting and finally Roberts mom had had enough and told Robert he would have to leave. I think Robert died emotionally that day.

Robert set it up for him and his mom to take a drive out to a farm to talk. A secluded area so that they would not be disturbed. He begged his mother to reconsider but her mind was made up. He wanted one last fuck and she said no. That's when he snapped. Robert beat and raped his mother over and over. She begged him to stop but he didn't. He put all of his rage into that act. Robert swears that he doesn't remember. He also claims that someone else did it. But that's not what his mom testified to in court. She contacted the police and Robert was arrested. She completely denied the accusation of incest. She told the court that Robert did it because she told him to leave if he could not get along with her new boyfriend. She testified in court that Robert was nothing but trouble and that he should be locked up. He was. Now Robert sits in prison waiting for the day that he will be released. That day will come.

HISTORY OF THE DEATH PENALTY IN MISSOURI

When I arrived at Potosi in 1995 the state was using lethal injection as the means by which executions were carried out. The first inmate to die by lethal injection was George "Tiny" Mercer. He belonged to motorcycle club and to celebrate his birthday one year his friends kidnapped a girl and gave her to him as a present. He used her in every unspeakable manner and when he was done he wanted the ultimate sick thrill and he killed her. His execution occurred on January 6, 1989.

By the time I arrived at the prison they had it down cold. The execution room and anteroom are in the bowels of the prison. They are located close to the medical area just in case. The execution room is ringed on three sides by a room and hallway. The room is used for the inmates witnesses. This could be immediate family or spiritual advisor. During many of the executions I witnessed this room was not used. Some inmates choose to leave this world alone. Those that I've discussed this with choose to not put their families through such a horrific ordeal. The reason the state chooses to put the family of the condemned in this room is obvious. The state wants a minimum of problems during these final hours. If there is going to be a negative out break they want it contained. The hallway that goes around the execution room is divided into two sections by heavy curtains. The type used by institutions everywhere to create separate rooms. One "room" is for the states witnesses. The media always applies for a seat as does the police and or prosecutors that handled the case. Many of the police that have witnessed executions have an emotional stake in the outcome. The crime that has led them to be here at this hour was usually exceptionally horrific. The other room is reserved for the victims witnesses. The separation between these rooms is more for show and the curtain is not fully closed. The information relayed to the witnesses by the assistant, the administering of the drugs and declaration of death, must be heard by all.

Immediately after the inmate is pronounced dead the inmates witnesses are removed from the execution area and are escorted back to the area from which they came. They are then escorted to their cars. The states witnesses are escorted away from the victims witnesses and are also escorted to their cars. The victims witnesses have the opportunity to speak to the press and many do. They have just witnessed the killing of a man. This man killed their family member and within minutes they are in front of glaring lights, cameras and have reporters questioning them about their experience. After the Q@A they are escorted back to the conference room to retrieve their belongings. We ask them if there is anything more we can do for them and then escort them to their cars. Another fellow Missourian has just been executed.

My experiences, although unique, go back to the beginnings of man. Punishment in the form of execution pre dates recorded history. From the codified dictates of Hammurabi to the Bloody Codes of Europe man has sought to kill man as punishment. In Missouri we began with hangings. These were done in public by the sheriff in the county where the crime was committed. Public executions were thought to have a deterrent effect. Next the state killed inmates by gas. The gas chamber method of execution was signed into law in 1937 by Governor Lloyd Crow Stark. The gas chamber was located at Missouri State Prison. These were some of the first private executions. The chamber cost $3,570.00 and consisted of two small cells on one side of the room and the chamber on the other side. One cell housed the condemned for his last few hours before the execution. The second cell was used for mixing the sulfuric acid that was used in the execution. This cell contained the crocks used to hold the sulfuric acid that was later placed under a metal perforated chair. The leather restraints that were used to bind the prisoner to the chair were also stored in this cell. In the center of the building was the air tight chamber painted white that held the two metal perforated chairs. Beneath the chairs were guides that held the crocks containing the sulfuric acid in place. When the order was given the warden pulled a lever outside of the chamber that dropped cyanide pellets into the crock. The mix of the cyanide and the sulfuric acid produced a lethal gas that slowly filled the chamber. Witness accounts of this type of execution reveals that many fought hard to the last breath. Although the condemned was told to breath deep many fought the gas as long as they could. They held their breath until they could hold it no longer similar to a drowning man. Knowing that the next breath would fill their lungs with poison panic would set in. The inmate would thrash about in the chair and pull against the restraints to try to distance himself from the toxic fumes. Finally when the lungs were about to explode he would inhale. The chamber by now would be full of the deadly mixture and his lungs would fill of it. The smell and taste of rotten eggs would fill his senses as his body started to respond to the poison. If in the panic he did not defecate he would now. The chamber would now be full of a rotten egg and feces smell. This would be one of his last experiences. As the lethal gas mixture permeates his body through his lungs the poison would take its toll. Within minutes he was dead. After the execution the lethal gas was extracted from the chamber and vented out a forty five foot pipe through the roof of the building. The inmate would be removed from the chamber and the chamber would be scrubbed down by an inmate.

In March of 1933 William Wright was convicted of first degree murder in the death of Dr. J.T. McCambell a druggist from the Kansas City area. In April 1936 John Brown was convicted for the shooting death of off duty policeman William Cavanaugh during an attempted robbery at a Kansas City tavern. They would have the infamous distinction of being the first to try this new method of execution. On March 4, 1938 as dignitaries and luminaries gathered the first use of the new method of execution was being prepared. It was a double execution. It was successful. The only other double execution to occur during the gas chambers history was in 1953. During the 1980's I was a dock worker for an electronics manufacturing company. I got to know many of the truck drivers that made the company a part of their regular route. One of these truck drivers, Bill, was a kind, older guy that had a very laid back attitude. Now, if you know truck drivers you know there are not many of these. One day as I was finishing loading Bills truck another driver came into my office to shoot the breeze and wait for his turn at being unloaded. I bid Bill farewell and started unloading the truck that had just pulled in. The driver of this truck asked me if I knew the story of the Greenlease boy. I had heard the story mentioned from time to time as I was growing up. My grandfather was a taxi driver in St. Louis for many years and my father also drove a taxi in his younger days. When Bill was a young man he also drove a taxi for a while in St. Louis. This was the story as it was told to me by the other driver. Bobby Greenlease was only six years old when he was kidnapped. The kidnappers demanded a large amount of money as ransom. The kidnappers also told the boys parents where to deliver the money. The police became involved as they always do. A high ranking policeman took the money and hailed a cab to deliver the money at the designated place. That cab driver was Bill. The money was supposedly delivered at the designated spot and then disappeared. Carl Austin Hall and Bonnie Brown Heady were arrested for the kidnapping. When Bobby Greenlease body was found they were then arrested for murder. Both were charged under the federal statutes for felony kidnapping and murder. Both were convicted. At that time the federal government had no means by which an execution could be carried out so Missouri agreed to perform the execution. On December 18, 1953 Missouri performed its second and last double execution. This execution was also significant in that Bonnie Brown Heady was the only woman executed by lethal gas. Bill and the policeman that delivered the ransom money told the federal authorities what had occurred that day. From the minute the policeman hailed Bills cab and through the route that they both agreed Bill drove to the drop point and back every second was scrutinized. It didn't add up. Too much time had passed. Although the federal authorities investigated they eventually dropped it. Who knows why. At that time the feds were more interested in commies is my guess. Over the years other truck drivers would talk about Bill and his connection with the case. Some would talk about his house as if it were a mansion that he could not possibly afford on a truck drivers wages. Others would discuss the trips that he and his wife would take through out the world and they did. One day I asked Bill about his role in the kidnapping and the rumors that somehow he and the officer had split the money. He told me it was all rumor and that if he and the officer did take the money and didn't deliver it it would surely have cost the young boy his life. He winked at me and told me to not believe everything I hear. From 1938 to 1965 the state of Missouri executed 39 prisoners by means of lethal gas. Three were executed for federal kidnapping, thirty for murder and six for rape. Twenty three were black and sixteen were white. The last execution by means of lethal gas was for the killing of a fifteen year old delivery boy at a St. Louis drugstore. Leo Lloyd Anderson holds the dubious distinction of being the last to smell the rotten egg odor of death prior to his passing on January 26, 1965. In 1968 a moratorium on capital punishment was invoked as a result of Furman vs. Georgia. On June 29, 1972, on a 5-4 vote, the U.S. Supreme Court ruled that the death penalty, as administered in Georgia, to be arbitrary and capricious and thus cruel and unusual punishment in violation of the eighth amendment. This suspended the death penalty nationwide. Arbitrary; depending on individual discretion (as of a judge), existing or coming about seemingly at random or by chance. Capricious; impulsive, unpredictable by whim, a turn of the mind. Because of this ruling all capital punishment inmates had their sentences changed to life in prison. The states had to revamp their laws in order to continue the killing. They did. On July 2, 1976 th United States Supreme Court ruled that the revised capital punishment laws of Florida, Georgia and Texas to be constitutional. A two part (bifurcated) system was put in place for capital punishment cases.

The first part would be the trial itself to find for guilt or innocence. The second part would be the penalty phase. Under this revised system the death penalty as a form of punishment was found to be not cruel and unusual. Missouri's revamped Capital Murder law became effective on May 26, 1977. It was modeled after those that had passed constitutional muster. The new Capital Murder law allowed for death as punishment to be sought as long as one of fourteen specifically listed aggravating circumstances are found to be part of the offense:

1. Prior capital murder convictions, or a history of serious assault convictions;

2. A second capital murder being commited at the same time;

3. Using a device in a public place that endangered persons other than the victim;

4. That the murder was commited for pay;

5. That the victim was a judicial officer or prosecutor, or had been one, and that the murder occurred during or because of the victim's excersize of his duties;

6. That the defendant hired another person to commit the murder;

7. That the crime "was outrageously or wantonly vile," involving "torture or depravity of mind";

8. That the victim was a working police officer, corrections officer or fireman;

9. That the murder was commited while the accused was in custody, or having escaped custody;

10. That the murder was commited to avoid, interfere with, or prevent the lawful arrest or custody of himself or another;

11. That the murder was commited during the commision or attempted commission of certain felonies;

12. That the murder victim was a witness or potential witness in any past or pending investigation or prosecution;

13. That the murder victim was a correctional employee or an inmate of a correctional institution;

14. That the murder victim was killed as a result of hijacking an airplane, train, ship, bus or other public conveyance.

Not every murder that has one of these attached aggravating circumstances results in the application for the death penalty. Prosecutors have much discretion. Budget constraints play a roll. Noteriety is also a factor and sometimes just dumb luck saves an inmate from the gallows. Just because an inmate has a sentence of death it doesn't mean he will be executed. Most are but some just happen to be at the right place at the right time. One year the Pope was visiting St. Louis. The govorner was able to arrange a private meeting with the pontiff. An execution was scheduled within the month. The Pope asked the governor to spare the man. He did. He commuted the man's sentence to life without parole. Right place, right time.

LARRY RICE

I've met damn few Christians in my life. I'm talking about true Christians. I've met a lot of people who have claimed to be Christian but are only Christian in the sense that they call themselves something. One of the few is The reverend Larry Rice. The chaplain that use to work at Potosi was once asked to justify his support of the death penalty. He quoted Jesus, "render unto Caesar that which is Caesars' and render unto God that which is Gods'. I guess what he meant was to obey the laws of man.

The way I see it is Jesus was talking about taxes. I didn't know that man created man. The "Christians" that I've met, at least most of them, are anti abortion and pro death penalty. If this is not blatant hypocrisy then hypocrisy doesn't exist. The Reverend Larry Rice was the exception. He was the main spiritual advisor for the C.P. inmates that gave a damn. He railed against the death penalty on his television show and was at the prison on the day of executions. If he was not inside watching and praying over their last breath then he was outside praying with the anti death penalty group. This group was always looked upon with derision as was Larry Rice by most of the staff at the prison. As an example; it was mid July, hot as hell and the good Reverend was getting ready to leave the prison at about three thirty in the afternoon. He had a flat tire on the prison parking lot. Now nothing goes on on the parking lot with out the institution knowing about it. The prison also has a mechanic on duty to help in just such a circumstance. The prison does not like for people to stay on the parking lot any longer than they have to so they help get people on their way. I did not witness this event but I heard the next day at the superintendents meeting that not only did no one lift a finger to help but the mechanic was told to let the Rev fix it himself while custody staff watched and laughed. I believe the quote was "how's it feel in hell Rev.". Good Christian people every one.

My job during most executions was to escort the victims witnesses to the execution. During one execution though I was needed to escort the condemned's 'witnesses. The wife of the inmate that was going to die was very emotional and the inmates brother was a cop. They needed someone who could talk down an emotional situation. The Reverend Larry Rice was the spiritual advisor for this execution. The inmate that was about to be killed was involved in a double homicide. He had been a shit most of his life. He'd been busted for burglary, minor assaults, drugs nothing heavy until the murders. The two men that were murdered were gay. A friend of the inmate that was about to die had been on a "date" with one of the men. They, along with another friend went to the gay couples home to burglarize it but the men were home. They went in anyway and a struggle ensued. They tied up the men, beat them, then stabbed and shot them. A short investigation led to the trio. All three were equally guilty. One of the men testified against the other two and pleaded guilty and received a parolable sentence. One of the men pleaded guilty and received life without parole. But the one guy that pleaded not guilty was about to lose his life. The inmates wife was hanging on the long shot chance that the courts or the governor would recognize the horrendous mistake the state was about to indulge in. She was shaking like a leaf and looked horrible. The good Reverend kept trying to get her to pray but her mind wandered and she kept repeating no this can't be happening and then she would cry softly. The reverend would try to engage her in talk of her husbands soul, it's all that would be left in a few minutes anyway, but she couldn't follow. The inmates brother was truly the most pathetic of them all. He talked to me and the Reverend about how he tried over the years to help his brother. How drugs and booze had taken him from the family. How when his brother got in trouble, nothing real serious, he would go to court and vouch for him. He told us about how he tried to talk to the prosecuting attorney that was handling the case and the prosecuting attorney wouldn't speak to him and him a cop. There was no great clamor for the death penalty in this case. The families of the murdered men kept to themselves. All three of the men were equally guilty.

I got the call that it was time to move the witnesses from the dock area. The victims witnesses are upstairs in an office and the inmates witnesses are on the dock. I stood up away from the table and told them it was time. They all joined hands to pray and it was at this moment that the inmates wife knew there would be no reprieve. As she stood to walk she couldn't. Her brother in law and the Reverend Larry Rice each took an arm and half carried half dragged her to the witnessing area and set her in a chair. As the blinds opened up she saw her beloved lying on the gurney a tube going into his arm. The inmate witness room is like a vacuum after the door is closed. All noise outside is muffled. The sounds on the inside are elevated. She moaned loudly as if the life was draining out of her. It was a sound that sent shivers up every one. You could feel it. As if this were his cue the Reverend put his arm around her and started to pray. His brother put his hand to the glass and bowed his head. In a low, muffled voice you could hear that the first drug was being administered. A few seconds later you could hear that the second drug was being administered. A few seconds after that the last drug was administered. Within a minute the muffled voice pronounced him dead. His wife was drained. She had no more emotion. I received word over my headset to move the witnesses back through the dock and to their cars immediately. The coroner had arrived early and some fool let him in. The reverend and brother took her again by the arms and half carried her out to their car. As they were pulling out the hearse was pulling in. There were crows on the fence and as the hearse backed in they flew away. All were equally guilty.

RALPH

He reminded me of an overgrown Larry Mondelo from Leave it to Beaver. He was complaining that his stomach was hurting him. He had been eating almost non-stop since this morning and now it was almost midnight. The grim reaper was standing outside of Ralph's door waiting. The closer it came to midnight the more nervous he got. Ralph's dance with death came about because of a politically ambitious prosecutor. "If this crime does not scream out for the death penalty than no crime does" was the mantra that led this parade. Ralph was socially inept but that didn't stop him from wanting a girlfriend. His wish was granted and he found himself in a relationship. It was the type of high anxiety situation where they are always on edge. The longer the relationship lasted the more Ralph got dependent on it. She felt just the opposite. She must have felt suffocated by this overgrown boy. To hear Ralph tell it he knew she was having an affair. This outraged him and gave him an over-whelming sense of insecurity. He didn't know what he would do if he lost her. When she had had enough she decided to call it quits. One night she told him that it was over. He couldn't or wouldn't accept this. She must have felt threatened because Ralph claimed that it was she that picked up the knife and attempted to stab him. He took it away from her and stabbed her in the neck. She fell to the floor bleeding. The autopsy revealed that he severed a major artery and cut her spinal cord. She was paralyzed and bled to death. The coroner said it could have taken up to four hours for her to die.

He panicked He said he didn't want to kill her. He knew what would happen when he was found out. In this paranoid panicked state he convinced himself that if he disposed of the body he may just get away with it. Now, if Ralph had called the police right away he would have been charged with second degree murder. A good defense attorney may have even gotten him voluntary manslaughter. The most time he would do would be twenty years. But Ralph decided to cut up his girlfriends body in pieces. He cut off her head, hands and legs from the knee down. He also cut off one foot. He put the parts in a bag and threw them in a pond and took the torso to a neighboring county and dumped it. This would make it hard for the authorities to make identification. The body was found and remained unidentified. A few days later Ralph went to the authorities to report his girlfriend missing. Ralph didn't have the fortitude to stand up to the questioning. He confessed right away and showed them where the remains were. GRIZZLY MURDER was the headline in the newspaper. The prosecutor expressed that this particularly brutal and heinous crime deserves the death penalty. He got it. At ten minutes to midnight the officer in charge told Ralph that it was time. His last walk was to begin. At this thought Ralph began to vomit. Like I said he had been eating all day. He started throwing up. And couldn't stop. It just kept coming. It reminded me of that scene from Steven Kings' Stand by Me where the fat kid is at the pie eating contest the barfarama.

MILTON

On more than one occasion capital punishment inmates have told me that those sentenced to death are political prisoners. In the United States is this a valid argument. Every justification that we the people have used to legitimize death as a punishment has been shown to be untrue. Of all of the murders committed only a small number of inmates ever receives the death penalty. Most families of the victims cry out for death, an eye for an eye and all that, only to be turned away disappointed for any number of reasons. The emotional reaction that a parent has when their child has been violated sexually is akin to the emotional reaction to a killing and yet we do not kill child molesters. This is proved by the vigilante acts by parents that have been caught on video tape or witnessed in court.

The day after an execution is always a tense day. More so than normal. During the superintendents meeting on the morning after an execution every incident that would normally be thought to be just typical inmate behavior is looked at more critically. We just killed one of theirs and now we must walk amongst them. We do not discuss the execution with them. There are no counselors to discuss with them their feelings about the killing. We do not have the luxury of recognizing them as emotional human beings. As a matter of fact the only psychologist assigned to the prison has been up all night to be available to the recently departed and is off the day after the execution to recuperate.

It was on one of these days that I walked into the inmate library and there were several inmates that had been sentenced to death working on their cases and discussing their recently departed friend. As I walked in to the library their discussion purposefully rose in pitch so that I would not miss what they were saying. One of the inmates, Milton, brought up the idea that they are political prisoners. I was curious as to their perspective on how they defined a political prisoner and asked what they meant. Had anyone been in the library except for the librarian I would have been in trouble. Discussing almost anything in depth or controversial with an inmate is a no-no. When ignorance reigns a complex thought is scary so it is prohibited. The librarian, a somewhat free spirit, was one of the few people that was not afraid of complex thought. If a person is making a decision in order to gain politically and just about all prosecutors do especially those that are in charge of deciding which cases are death penalty cases then their decision is based on politics. This was the gist of their argument. I explained to them that this stretches the definition of political prisoner outside of the realm for which it was intended. I went on to explain that a political prisoner is punished for their political beliefs, thoughts and actions and that you all are being punished for killing someone. Milton went on to explain that if the law is applied fairly across the board my argument had merit but as long as the courts i.e. politicians continued to change the rules leaving dead prisoners in its wake then what punishment is right today may not be true tomorrow. That what political beliefs, thoughts and actions that exist today might not exist tomorrow. Punishment is not the issue he said but the death penalty is. Either all killing must be met with killing or none must. If you pick and choose then it is arbitrary and the state is killing the inmate based strictly on its beliefs and not for any other reason. This is political. Therefore capital punishment inmates are political prisoners not just prisoners. I agreed that their argument had merit but I was not completely convinced. I told them to keep working on it.

Milton grew up in a poor rough neighborhood. His role models were the drug dealers, thieves, robbers, pimps and whores of the street. His first recorded crime was when he was eighteen and got busted for burglary. I'm sure he had some juvenile records but those were off limits. He was arrested for burglary a second time within two years and was sentenced to a year in jail. He was released a few months early and before the year was out was arrested again. This time he was arrested for robbery first degree and stealing a motor vehicle. He was sentenced to nine years in prison. His first bit (sentence) was a year or less that's why he went to jail anything over a year and you usually go to prison. He was twenty five years old and his life as society defines it was over. If you ask politicians about which role models in their lives inspired them almost to a person they will tell you about someone. A role model is what all people seek. If the role model is a criminal then it is likely that you will model this behavior. Even animals in the wild must do this to survive. The baby must model its parent. By 1986 Milton was out of prison and with his formal education (prison) behind him he was back to doing what his modeling taught him. A friend of his told him about some electronic equipment that could be stolen from a residence. The friend explained to him that if they were seen by the owners that he would have to kill them because the owners knew him and he wasn't going back to prison. Milton was fine with that, his life was over anyway, so he went along. They went to the residence and the people were home. They knocked on the door and when the owner answered the door they forced their way in. They assaulted the owner and his girlfriend. They then tied them up. Milton strangled the girl until she passed out. He then hit the man over the head with a wrench and knocked him unconscious or so he thought. As they were gathering up the electronic equipment the girl came to. Miltons buddy then stabbed her to death. He then went to the owner and stabbed him. First Miltons buddy got arrested. The witness that came forward with the information was contacted by Milton and Milton told her that it was he Milton that did the killing. The investigation revealed that the stabbing of the girl is what killed her and that the prior strangling had no bearing on her death. The owner died from the blow to the head that Milton delivered and the stabbing contributed to his death. Both committed a murder. I hate to state that any murder is run of the mill but in the big scheme of things that was what this was. Unfortunately, this type of crime happens everyday and the vast majority of the killers never get the death penalty. Milton did. Milton was charged with two counts of first degree murder. He went to a jury trial and the jury found him guilty. The jury sentenced Milton to life in prison without parole in the murder of the girl but was deadlocked on punishment for the murder of the owner. The judge sentenced him to death. I talked to Milton from time to time during the next year or so. I asked him once how it was going and he said he was scared. He said that he had worked his ass off on his case but it didn't look good. I asked him about his argument on political prisoner status and he said it hadn't changed. In another place at another time he would have been punished for killing but he wouldn't have to die for it. In March 1998 I watched as Milton laid on the gurney the I.V. tubes running from his arms. The I.V. contains normal saline so the veins will expand. The assistant recited the process of death for all to hear and follow. Through his headset he listened as the mechanic explained what he was doing and he repeated this to all of the witnesses. The first button pushed releases the first drug, Sodium Pentathol, that renders the inmate unconscious. The assistant stated the first drug was being administered. Within seconds Miltons eyes closed. The second button pushed releases the next drug, Pancronium Bromide (Pavulon), that stops the breathing. The assistant stated that the second drug was being administered. Also, within seconds Melton's body tries to take in air and expels what air is left. This causes the chest to heave slightly. This is the last visible action of the body. The third button is pushed to release the last drug, Potassium Chloride, this will stop the heart. The assistant states that the third drug is being administered. Milton is just lying there as if asleep. Time passes. The assistant states that the execution is complete. In 2003 the ninth circuit federal court ruled that it was unconstitutional for a judge to hand down a sentence of death in a situation where the jury was deadlocked on its decision. The death penalty can only be handed down by a jury of peers. Another place and another time.

AN ENEMA BEFORE DYING

Truman Capote walked in in all his flamboyance only he was six feet two inches tall and about two hundred sixty pounds. He wore a 1940's style hat, tinted glasses, and draped his coat over his shoulders a la Truman. Thus began one of the most bizarre evenings of execution that I had experienced.

As soon as a victim's witness to an execution arrives at the prison the escort is notified. We meet them just outside the front door. Prior to them entering the prison we use a hand held metal detector and go over their body just to make sure they are not trying to do the states job. Truman had on more jewelry than Mr. T. and set off the wand several times. He asked why this was necessary and I told him that it was routine. He then started in with the questions that would fill my night. Did anyone ever bring in a gun and try to shoot the condemned before an execution he asked. My answer was that we would not reveal what went on during an execution but no this has never happened. You handle a victims witness with kid gloves. I told him that prior to the execution his personal belongings would be placed in a locked box and that he would probably feel more comfortable if he locked his jewelry in his car. He asked why we had to do this. When I told him it was for the safety and security of all involved he wanted to know specifics. I told him that in a prison we have to prepare for any situations that may occur. Like what; he asked. This was going to be a difficult night. He did not act like any other victim's witness or any witness I had escorted during an execution. His curiosity was going to be a challenge. I gave him an example of the lost wallet. I told him that on the off chance he lost his wallet while inside and an inmate found it the inmate would have identification that he may be able to use to escape. I told him the same thing could happen with his car keys. He decided to put most of his jewelry in his car before he entered. I got him inside and the long night began. I looked into his relationship with victim and found that he was a distant relative and that he had not seen the victim in years. The Missouri Department of Corrections does everything it can to make sure that if any family member wants to be present during the execution we will try to accommodate. Somehow he found out about the pending execution and decided to see what it was all about. Every witness that I have had to an execution is low key. The mood is somber. The only exception was Truman. He wanted to know everything. How were the inmates treated on death row. What did they eat. Did rape really happen. Did we beat them. Did rape really happen. There was a pattern forming here. He wasn't jovial but he wasn't in mourning and he talked of his relative and the memories he had as a child and I got the impression that he had not seen his relative for a long time. Why do we do this, why do we do that. The questions went on and on. Finally, it was time to go to the execution. I thought that the seriousness of what he was about to encounter would shut him up. No chance. When the curtain opened to reveal the condemned he asked rhetorically if that was the bastard that did the deed. I think the questions covered his nervousness. When the assistant went through the routine of the administering of drugs he wanted to know what the drugs were. When it was all over I was exhausted. We gathered his possessions and I began to escort him to his car. The last question he asked me before he left was if the state forced the inmate to have an enema before the execution. I told him I didn't know.

ERIK

"Did you know Mr. Minard that blood and fire are the most power-ful forces on earth." This is how the first conversation I had with Erik started. I had just started my new assignment in the special needs unit (snu) the day before. I had to prioritize my contacts with my new inmate-patients and Erik was one of the first. Sitting across the desk from me in the counseling office Erik reminded me of an old time wrestler. Premature bald, overweight and smelled like a rank locker room. He wore a filthy t-shirt and cut off sweat pants the bandage on his leg,also filthy, oozed a mixture of blood and whatever. Erik became a priority because he had just been released from medical, yet again, because he had reburned the hole in his leg. When he got upset he would take a bic lighter and flame on he would hold it to a spot on his leg, same spot every time, until he could not stand it anymore or pass out. This last time he passed out. "Blood and fire Mr. Minard don't you think. Blood gives life is life and fire destroys all. What I say is true ain't it." I asked Erik why he burned himself and he explained to me that when the "ladies" are in his head the only thing that removes them is fire. Erik was raised in rural Jefferson county Missouri. He told me that his father was an asshole. While in high school his father taught him to work on cars. By his admission he was a very good mechanic. Socially he was the butt of the school. If someone needed help working on their car he was a "friend" other than that he was ostracized. Like all young men he wanted to fit in and have a girlfriend. He told me "people fucked with me" I asked him to give me an example. "One night" he started, "A couple of people from school showed up at my house because they needed help with their car. There was a girl with them that I liked. As I started working on the car they said that if I got it running that the girl would fuck me." At the thought Erik smiled and looked at me. "I busted my ass fixing their car. I used my parts and my tools. I stole beer from my dad for us to drink. I smoked my pot with them. I got the car running. I went inside and got cleaned up while they sat outside drinking my beer and smoking my pot. When I walked outside they were all in the car and I walked up to the door to get in. The girl in the car looked up at me and started laughing. She said 'You dumbass I wouldn't fuck you for a million bucks' they all laughed and then took off. I got in my car to follow them but didn't. I just drove around and got more pissed. I was driving real fast down the road and just thought about jumping out while the car was going. Then I thought about opening the drivers door and sticking my leg out. I did this and started dragging my foot on the ground. It would catch and hurt like hell. Then I hit the door on a telephone pole and my leg got kinda smashed and that really hurt like hell but I kinda felt better." Erik, like most of the inmates incarcerated at P.C.C., is in for murder. The story he told me was replicated many times in one fashion or the other all the while he was in school. Get used, get pissed off self mutilate. His peer group was off limits so he befriended older people. It was a decision that would destroy the lives of two deeply religious elderly women and their families and send Erik to prison for the rest of his life. Both of his victims lived alone. Erik turned into a handyman of sorts for several elderly people in the area. The rage must have been building in Erik for some time. He went to his first victims house to help with some things around the house and he brought with him a very large hunting knife. While inside the house something inside Erik must have snapped. The self mutilating must not have been enough anymore. The rage needed an outlet. Erik started stabbing the woman and she blessed him. When he was done he cleaned up the area and set the house on fire. He asked me once how she could have said god bless you Erik as he was stabbing her. Erik became a suspect and then confessed to avoid the death penalty. He was sentenced to life in prison. His other victim he beat to death with a sawed off baseball bat. He then set her house on fire. In what can only be described as gross incompetence this murder was originally ruled accidental even though her purse was missing, her drivers license was found in a ditch and her credit card was found on a parking lot.

The guilt weighed heavy on Erik. While in prison the self mutilating increased. Even though he was severely mentally ill the prison system did nothing for him. He was raped numerous times and made to do all sorts of perversions. He would tell the authorities only to recant under threat of death. This happens all the time. Eventually the guilt won out and Erik asked to speak with the prosecutor in the county that the second murder occurred. He agreed to confess if they did not seek the death penalty. Erik was tried for the second murder and was convicted and given a second life sentence. He was living the hell that most people feel an inmate needs to live. He told me once that other than the murders his biggest regret was not going to court and fighting the charges. He knew that in the county he committed the murders in when found guilty he would have been sentenced to death and his pain would now be over.

INVESTIGATIONS

Christmas time in prison is an extremely depressing time. The negative impact of the holidays on the streets is magnified on the inside. For this reason the inmates in the SNU are even more closely monitored. Catholic Charities is one of the few groups that will involve themselves in the lives of inmates. The SNU inmates get special attention. During December Catholic Charities starts sending in donated goods for the SNU. These items all have to pass the safety and security test. The items are usually no more than socks, which they desperately need, deodorant, toothpaste, toothbrushes maybe a cap of some kind, just the basics.

The weekend before Christmas there is a party. The only Christmas party at Potosi. The nuns come in and some staff even show up. We had some success integrating a few of the SNU inmates into jobs along side the general population inmates. Half way through the party the inmates that were at work came in from their jobs. We could tell that something was wrong. They came in and went straight to their cells and requested to be locked down. They are allowed to do this especially if they are feeling depressed or out of control but there was a party going on. One they have been looking forward to all year. We started talking to them and found out that one of them had just been raped at work. There are some really sick fucks in prison. Unfortunately this is a common occurrence. Many mentally ill people in prison are used this way. Pretty soon the word

spread about what had happened. To say it put a damper on the fes-
tivities is an understatement. We went from partying to counseling.
I'm glad the nuns were there to help. Since it was a Saturday there
were no investigators at the prison. I escorted the inmate to medical
for his examination. Medical confirmed that he was raped. The rapist had used butter as a lubricant. I contacted the head of security to
report what had happened and he was reluctant to do anything.
After I had explained that everybody in the SNU knew about what
had happened he had the rapist placed in the hole pending an investigation. I spent the next two hours putting together the report.
Merry Christmas in the SNU. On Monday the investigators office
got my report and started an investigation. I was asked to be a witness to the CVSA this is a computer voice stress analysis test. How
they determine if a person is lying is by asking a series of test questions in which the person being questioned tells the truth and also
purposefully lies. An example would be; Are you in prison? Yes. Is
your mother a man? Yes. The first question is true and the second
question is a lie. The inmate could not follow these simple direc-
tions. But the CVSA was given anyway. The investigators in their
infinite wisdom had found out that this inmate had accused an
inmate in the past of rape. During the course of the first rape investigation they had determined that according to the results of the
CVSA the inmate was being deceitful. Also, after his first rapist was
released from the hole he recanted. The CVSA was a joke but they
used the results anyway to determine he was again be deceitful. During questioning the victim was asked if it was he that put the butter
on his anus. He said yes that the rapist told him to or he would hurt
him. End of investigation. If he put the booty butter on himself it
was mutual consent. The inmate in the hole was claiming all along

it was mutual. Now he could either go back to the SNU and forget about it or take a write up for sexual contact. He went back to the SNU. Investigations in prison are always a foregone conclusion. They exist strictly to protect the department. The CVSA is the cheapest, most unreliable piece of truth gathering equipment there is. Flipping a coin is as reliable but they use it as if it were the same as a lie detector test.

SNU

My final assignment at Potosi was in the SNU, special needs unit. This unit housed the most uncontrollable. The worst of the worst, those that must be kept. It was the most personally rewarding job I had but a career disaster. The snu got its start because an inmate killed an officer. All I can give you is second hand information on why the murder occurred. It was a hit. An officer pissed off some inmates at Jefferson City Correctional Center. They then convinced a feeble minded inmate to kill him and he did. As the story is told the inmate was beat within an inch of his lifeby staff members, taken into the underground tunnels and handcuffed to an overhead pipe. The order was then given that he was not to sleep. If he was not feeble minded before the assault he certainly was by the time I encountered him at the SNU. The inmate was given the death penalty but the governor wanted to make sure it didn't happen again. I'm not sure if it was for the safety of the officers or if it was to make sure that the retards couldn't be used. The guy was so mentally fucked up that the governor eventually commuted his sentence to life without parole. The snu housed developmentally disabled inmates. A developmental disability occurs prior to age twenty two. It covers mental retardation, bi-polar disorder, schizophrenia, personality disorder as well as some others. Many of the inmates suffered from personality disorder. To me this is the most fascinating and hardest to control. The personality disordered inmate reacts in an extreme way no matter what the situation. The reaction to a perceived slight will be the same reaction to a critical incident. Their reactions though will vary. Some become assaultive some self mutilate and some are shit smearers. The shit smearers are by far the nastiness. The Picassos of poop I call them. They will paint their cells and if that doesn't get them the attention they want then they start to feast. How some of them make it through the court system and are convicted shows just how dedicated our judicial system is. As far as our judicial system is concerned there is only one mental abnormality, insanity. A system of justice that is based on the best mental health theories available in the nineteenth century is about par for the course. Why don't we just go back another couple of decades and blame it on demonic possession. Idiots. Most of the inmates in snu must be kept. They are violent, extremely hard to control and have no place else to go. For the most part their families have abandoned them. Many of their family members have similar mental health problems. When an inmate in SNU does get a visit it can be either a blessing or a curse.

Bens' visit turned out to be a curse. Ben and his brother robbed a place or should I say Bens brother robbed a place while Ben was standing there. He was tried and convicted and sent to prison. He was so mentally retarded that he could not follow orders. Although initially sent to a low level prison, since he couldn't follow orders he was eventually rolled to Potosi. His mother came for a visit one day and told him that he had been gone long enough and that it was time he came home. His mother also had issues. When Ben got back out on the yard he nonchalantly walked up to the fence and started to climb over it. Ben is now an escape risk.

The savant of the SNU was Bobby. He also came from a family that had problems. Bobby loved the carnival and circuses. One day when the carnival was in town Bobby just hooked up with them and off he went. Bobby also loved women and eventually crack cocaine and booze. Another carnie, a woman, his "girlfriend" and he were out getting high in southern Missouri. They ran out of money. The girl got her hands on a gun gave it to Bobby and told him if he loved her he would get her more money for dope. Bobby took the gun, it had no bullets, walked into a liquor store and told him he wanted money. The owner gave him some money and Bobby left. Bobby had to walk back to the carnival because he had no car. The police picked him up on the way. Even though Bobby's I Q is around 70 his artwork is phenomenal. His artwork is similar to another Bobby, Robert Crumb. The artist from the late 60's and 70's. Probably the most recognized pieces of Robert Crumbs is the Keep on Trucking man and Mr. Natural. He also did the X-rated cartoon Fritz the Cat. The SNU sure had its cast of characters.

Unfortunately for the inmates in the SNU getting treatment for their problems was hit and miss, mostly miss. To state that the resources provided were meager would be an understatement. The mental health guy in charge was an administrator. He may have practiced psychology at some time in his past but if he was there two hours a week for counseling sessions that would have been about it. He drove across the state to work He spent a lot of time in his hotel room. He seemed to be not feeling well a lot. My supervisor was a devil worshiper that loved Marilyn Manson and kept snakes as pets. Like I said the SNU had its cast of characters. The inmates didn't have a chance. I was unceremoniously transferred from the SNU due to threats against me from other staff members. Like I said, the inmates in the SNU are violent and unpredictable. How you treat them and how you handle them could be the difference between life and death. For this reason I tried to keep the redneck cowboy officers and their supervisors from coming in to the unit. They were to stupid to recognize the volatility of the situation even though one of their own was killed by the inmate that started the unit. Go figure. One of their best and brightest came into the unit at midnight one night to question an inmate about a rumor that he was making shanks. The inmate did have a reputation for such behavior. The inmate said he didn't know anything about it. The officer then took out a piece of gum, unwrapped it, and threw the wrapper on the floor. He then told the inmate to pick up the wrapper. The inmate told him he didn't want any trouble. The officer told him he had till the count of three to pick it up or he would make him pick it up. The inmate picked up the wrapper and the officer left. Every inmate in the unit heard what went on. The next day was hell. I didn't know why. The inmates were as out of control as I had ever seen. My supervisor kept me away from the unit as much as he could doing paperwork in the office. He and the mental health guy tried to cover it up. When I found out what happened I got pissed. I filed a report on what I found out then they got pissed. As I was leaving the prison a few days later the officer that started it all came up to me in the administration building and told me to watch my back. This kind of threat in a maximum security prison I am not going to ignore. For all the good it did I reported it. Then I was transferred.

IN THEIR OWN WORDS

Throughout the course of my work I have been sent writings, poems, pictures and various correspondence. I write about my experiences and the unique position I have found myself in but nothing can convey the essence of the criminal and the prison system more than their own words. What they think and how they think. The following chapter is an autobiography written in the inmates own words. It captures the essence of a pedophile. I will make no comment as I will let it speak for itself.

I was born in St. Louis Missouri on December 27, 1967. When I was eighteen months old my father left my mother and I, never to return. At approximately three and one half years old I was taken from my mother for unknown reasons and placed in a foster care. My three month old brother was also taken. We were placed in two different homes and I have not seen my brother since. I didn't realize at the time that I would always feel an empty spot in my life for the companionship of a brother.

I don't remember much about the first foster home but at the second one there was five other children. The only other boy there was mentally retarded. He was about two or three years older than me and he was my only friend. The two other foster children were girls. One of the girls was about two years older than me and the other about my age. My foster parents had two girls of their own. One of them was a year younger than me and the other five or six years older.

I can remember several incidents while living in this foster home. First of all all the foster kids were terrified of the foster Dad including me. I don't remember why exactly. I just remember we would set on the couch and watch out the window for him to come home. As soon as he pulled into the driveway we would head for our rooms or outside to avoid him.

One of the reasons we were afraid of him was because of this game (for the lack of a better word) that he would make just the foster kids play. By singling us out he made us feel like we were there solely for his amusement. The rules of the game went something like this. We would have to line up in the living room and one by one we would have to run through the kitchen and out the back door past him while he shot us with rubber bands from his post at the back of the kitchen. If we made it past him without being hit then we were free to go outside. If we got hit we had to get back in line. We had to play the game until we got past him without being hit by the rubber band.

One night I went over to one of the foster sister's bed (the one that was the same age as me). I pulled down her pajamas and underwear and started kissing her on the mouth and rubbing her vagina. Then I put my finger in her vagina. She started crying really hard so I stopped. I was afraid my foster parents would hear. Somehow they found out what I did and made me sleep in the bathtub the next night. That's all the punishment I remember them giving me.

My foster father and I spent a lot of time in the house alone. He would watch TV while lying on the floor. He made me lay down with him with my head between his knees like a choke hold. He would make me stay like that sometimes for what seemed like hours. Sometimes I would fall asleep like that. I never understood the purpose of this act. I don't recall any sexual contact or anything. It's just a strange memory.

When I started Kindergarten I was in a behavior class. The teacher used to put me in an empty room with an empty cardboard box. She made me kick the box until I calmed down.

One day on the way home from school the school bus stopped by another school to pick up more kids. When the bus driver got off the bus I went up to the front and released the emergency brake. Our bus rolled into a bus parked in front of it. When we got to my foster home the bus driver told my foster mother what I had done. She in turn told my foster dad when he got home. He hit me on the left side of my head with a board. He had to take me to a hospital because my head started bleeding. He told the doctors I had fallen down the stairs. I just stared at him and kept my mouth shut. This is the only time I remember him hitting me.

During the first two years in foster care I was allowed to see my Mom once a month. During one of these visits she informed me that we would not be allowed to see each other anymore. She said she had signed papers so that the social service people could find me a good family to live with. I started crying and begged her not to give me away. I told her I still loved her even if she didn't love me. I promised her I would be a good boy. I didn't see my mother again until 1990.

Around December of 1974 when I was seven I went to live with a family that was thinking of adopting me. They had two daughters of their own. One was about five and the other one was in high school. The younger daughter and I got along real good. When I got in trouble at school the father would take me out to the tool shed and spank me with a belt. The five year old would always hold up for me and beg him not to hurt me. Always after the spanking he would make me take a shower with him. He would keep the water ice cold. I don't the reason for these showers. There never was any sexual contact that I can remember.

In April of 1975 they sent me back to the foster home. They claimed I was too hyper for them and that I was always getting into trouble at school.

When I arrived back at the foster home the father said that I was so much trouble that no body wanted me and that no one would ever want to adopt me. He said I was stuck with him and that I might as well get used to it.

In July of 1975 my foster parents told me that some friends were coming down from St. Louis and that we were all going to the park for a picnic. At the park the people from St. Louis seemed to pay more attention to me than any of the other children. The next day my foster Mom told me the people weren't really friends but some people that were looking for a boy to adopt. She said they wanted to take me to the movies so that we could get to know each other better.

I started seeing them about once a week. Around September they asked me if I would like to come live with them and be their son. I said yes I would love to come live with you and be your son.

On the morning of September 22, 1975, waiting for my new parents to pick me up, I was very nervous. I hadn't slept all night. I had to go to school that day but when I got home My new parents would be picking me up to take me to my new home. That day at school seemed like it took forever. When they got there I was setting on the couch looking out the window. I said good bye to my foster Mom. The other kids were outside playing and my foster Dad was at work.

When we got to my new home I was shown my new room. I thought it was the neatest thing to have my own room because I had never had my own room before. That night I had a hard time getting to sleep. For the first time I felt secure and loved. I finally felt like I belonged someplace.

I started school the following Monday. I was placed in a special school because of my behavior and my learning disability.

For about the first six months I would wake up in the night scared and call out for my mother. She would come in and set with me until I fell back asleep.

Sometime between the ages of seven and ten I started wetting the bed, on purpose.

I don't know why except I liked the way it felt.

I craved attention, good or bad, I didn't care which as long as I got as much attention as possible. This meant that I was always getting in trouble. I was kept in the special school all through grade school. Many times I would see the teachers helping some other kid and get very jealous. I would jump up and start destroying the classroom. Usually by the time the teacher could restrain me the room would look like a tornado had hit it. I would throw anything I could get my hands on and bite, kick and scratch the other children as well as the teacher.

At first my new parents and I got along real good. My father and I would play Monopoly and watch Shirley Temple and Abbot and Costello movies on TV every Saturday afternoon. Sometimes my Dad would come into my bedroom in the mornings and lay down on the bed with me. I liked it when he laid down with me. I felt loved and protected at those times. There was nothing sexual in this action just my Dad trying to connect with me.

Within the first year I made friends with two kids that lived behind us. One was a boy a year older than me. He was also adopted so we had that in common. The other kid was four years younger than me.

One day the older boy and I were playing in his back yard. I was about nine at this time. A boy about seventeen, which neither of us knew, came into the yard and asked if he could play too. Somehow we ended up in the garage. The guy started kissing me on the mouth. I told him to stop or I'd tell my Mom. He grabbed my crotch and said if I told anyone he'd cut off my dick. Then he told us to pull down our pants. We did as he said. He then performed oral sex on first one of us then the other.

My Mom had seen us go into the garage and asked what we were doing in there. At first I refused to tell her but she kept asking. She threatened to call my friends Mom. I started crying and told her what had happened. She asked me why I hadn't told her right away. I told her he had threatened to cut off our dicks if we told. I told her I was afraid she would get mad at me and send me back to the foster home. She told me she would always love me. She didn't always like the things I did however. She said I could stay with them as long as I wanted. She called my friends Mom and told her what happened. I don't know if anything ever happened to the guy. I never saw him again.

It was right after this incident that I met my second victim. He was about three years old. He had blond hair and blue eyes (the perfect combination.) He had just moved in across the street. I immediately fell in love with him. He was real shy. It took me almost a year to get him to trust me enough to victimize him.

One day we were playing hide and go seek. I led him into some bushes where no one could see us. He said he had to go to the bathroom. I told him to just go right there in the bushes. He started to pull down his shorts. I told him not to pull them down but to go in his pants. He said if he did all the kids would make fun of him. I sat down on the ground and told him to set on my lap. I told him to pee on my lap. After he did I started kissing him and rubbing his crotch. I pulled down his shorts and started playing with his penis. He wanted me to stop and I asked him if he wanted me to tell all the other kids that he had peed in his pants like a little baby. I made him take off his pants and let me touch him anywhere I wanted. I told him I loved him. I then performed oral sex on him. I warned him again that I'd tell all the kids he peed his pants like a baby if he told anyone. Then I let him get dressed and got him home before the other kids saw his wet pants. I repeated this action numerous times over the next five years until his family moved away.

Around the time that I was victimizing the neighbor boy I was told this would be my last year in special school. I learned that regular schools didn't have time out rooms like the special school so they wouldn't be able to discipline me that way anymore. The time out room was a small concrete room that they locked me in when I was out of control. My new teacher wanted me to learn how to control my behavior on my own. The teachers at the special school also would hold me down when I was out of control which I became to like. Again any attention was good negative or otherwise and physical attention was what I came to want, need and expect.

In about1981 or 1982 I started Junior High School. Although I was no longer going to a special school I was attending a special resource classroom. I was still considered learning and behaviorally challenged.

During my second year of Junior High I became close to my teacher. She worked for an organization called S.L.A.R.C. which was short for St. Louis Association for Retarded Citizens. One day she asked me if I would like to volunteer at a weekend camp that she worked at on Saturdays. For the next five years this opportunity afforded me numerous victims.

The first Saturday I worked at the camp I helped out in a group that had a five year old boy in it. He wasn't mentally retarded but he did have a severe behavior problem. He reminded me a lot of myself when I was that age.

At the end of the day they had a meeting of all the counselors. At the meeting the head counselor asked me if I would volunteer to work one-on-one with the five year old. I asked my teacher if I could do it. She was reluctant at first but then agreed to let me. I immediately fell in love with him. He was not one of my victims but I did have fantasies about him. I fantasized kidnapping him, molesting him and then killing him so he couldn't tell.

A few years and numerous victims later I was given my own group to lead at the camp. There was a seven year old boy in my group. He was extremely shy. He went to a school near my home to go swimming. One day I cornered him in the locker room while the others were busy swimming. I started kissing him while I fondled his penis. I took off his swim suit and performed oral sex on him. I continued to molest him numerous times while he was in my group.

About the time I started working at the camp my relationship with my father started going downhill. We could seldom talk without arguing.

During the first summer I worked at the S.L.A.R.C. camp I stayed on the premises all summer. On one occasion the nurse at the camp asked me to baby-sit for her three year old son. He slept in my bed. I knew he had a bed wetting problem. I purposefully gave him lots to drink before bed. Sometime during the night he woke me up and said he had to pee. I told him the bathroom was broken and that he'd have to go outside in the woods. He asked me if I would go with him. I told him "No I'm going back to sleep." He started crying and said he was too scared to go out there alone. I told him since he was too scared to go outside to just pee in his pajamas. He had no choice so he peed in his pants right there in the bed. After he peed his pants I told him to take them off and I performed oral sex on him. I then turned him over and massaged his but until he fell asleep. I continued to molest him and his three year old brother repeatedly that year.

In January of 1986 I started dating one of the counselors at the camp. I was eighteen and she was twenty-six. She was my first sexual experience with an adult. I found the experience overrated and sexually unfulfilling.

I always had trouble holding jobs (with the exception of babysitting and the job at the camp.) I would either get bored or just quit or get fired. So I started going to a Junior College. I majored in child psychology and child development. In late April one of my classes went on a field trip to Wisconsin for a weekend long lecture. As we boarded the bus I spotted a teacher I didn't know get on the bus with her five year old daughter. I sat with the girl on the bus and she asked me if I would read to her. We went to the back of the bus so we wouldn't disturb anyone. Just being close to her excited me.

Later that night at dinner I excused myself to go to my cabin to get my coat. I asked the girl if she could go along with me. Her Mom said it was OK. As soon as I got her to the cabin I took her into the bedroom and took off her panties. She started crying right away but didn't try to stop me. I started kissing her and rubbing her vagina. I laid her back and performed oral sex on her Then I dressed her and when I was done I went into the bathroom and masturbated. When I came out of the bathroom she was jumping up and down on the bed like nothing had happened. I took her back to the dining hall and went on to the first lecture.

Later that evening everyone was setting around a campfire signing songs. The girl and her Mom was there too. I asked the girl if she wanted to come over and set on my lap. She started shaking and crying like she had seen a ghost. Then two men came up to me and said they wanted to talk to me in the office. As we started toward the office I saw a police car parked in front. I knew then that the girl must have told her Mom what I'd done.

Two policemen were waiting for me. They told me the girl had told on me. They asked me why I did it. At first, I denied it but then I admitted what I'd done. I told them there were other victims in St. Louis. They drove me to a bus station and told me to leave town. Later I found out they thought that I'd only kissed her.

When I got back to St. Louis I called my Mom and told that I'd kissed a girl and was told to leave the lecture. I asked her pick me up and she said she would. When she got there she started asking me questions. I told her I was tired that I'd been up for twenty-four hours and that I'd answer her questions in the morning.

The next morning the phone woke me up. I could hear my Mom on the phone denying she knew anything about me molesting any kids. Then she came into my room. I was crying. I told her it was all true and that I was glad that it was finally out in the open. Then she told me that the phone call had been Family Services and that they were sending someone over to talk to me. The police in Wisconsin had called Family Services and reported me.

When the lady from Family Services came I told her about seventeen children that I had molested. She left but returned about three days later with a policeman. They took me to the Police Station where I repeated everything I had told the Family Services lady. I was arrested and charged with ten counts of sodomy. My Mon got me a lawyer and he plea bargained it down to two counts of sodomy and one count of sexual assault. I was sentenced to ten years in prison. The ten years were suspended pending five years of probation and the sexual assault was dropped to eighteen months in prison.

After I was paroled on May 2,1988 I started going to the Master's and Johnson's Clinic in St. Louis. They gave me a drug called Depro Pravera. It was supposed to slow down my sexual desires. It helped a little but wasn't really very effective. I went to a clinic to get my meds where there were children all around. If I had remained in custody I wouldn't have had that access to kids and the drugs would have been more help.

About two weeks after I was released from prison I started a job with a private construction company. My boss had seven children. Even though he knew why I had been in prison one day he asked me to baby-sit for him. He needed someone to watch his two year old daughter. I told him that as a condition of my parole I wasn't allowed to be with children alone. He must have needed a baby-sitter pretty bad because he told me he didn't care. He said he needed my help and if I refused I would be fired.

That night I molested the little girl. I then went home and took every pill in the house. I wanted to kill myself. I was so frustrated. I knew I was fighting a battle that I couldn't win. I woke up in the hospital the next day. I called the little girls Mother and told her what I'd done. Then I called my parole officer and told him what I'd done. My parole was revoked of course. In 1989 I was returned to prison. This time to finish my ten year sentence.

In 1990 my real mother came to prison to visit me. She had contacted my adopted parents and they told her I was in prison. She told me I also had a sister that I had not known about. Since then she has also come to visit me.

What I want to say with this writing is that I blame the system for me molesting that last little girl. They let me out when they knew what I was. What they need to know is that what I did has no comparison to what I fantasize about doing. The following is an example of my fantasies. Given the opportunity fantasy could become reality and that opportunity will come in ten years or less.

My Fantasy:

I'm in a store looking for my next victim when I spot two children, a boy and a girl, with their mother. They appear to be around three or four years old.

I go out to the car and wait for them to come out. Then I follow them home. From there I go to a store and buy supplies. I go home and wait for a few hours until it's late into the night. While I'm waiting I shave all the hair off my body except for my head. I plan to cover my head with a shower cap when the time comes. I put on a wet suit like you'd wear to go deep sea diving that I'd bought for the occasion. Then I put my clothes on over the suit.

Around 1:00 am I'm setting in my car in front of the house where the kids live. I take off the second layer of clothes and put on heavy winter socks over my shoes. I put on the shower cap. I take out my gun with the silencer from my gym bag. I walk around to the back of the house. I take a crowbar from my bag and pry open the back door. After walking in the back door I listen for a few minutes making sure I haven't woken anyone. I walk into the parents bedroom and shoot both of them in the head twice each. Now that the parents are dead I feel the power of the rush knowing I can do whatever I want with the kids. I feel invincible. I know I'll never get caught because there will be no witnesses.

I check out the rest of the house and in doing so find an infant in his crib in another bedroom sleeping. I don't want the police to think I have a conscience so I shoot the baby too. I made a self imposed rule that everyone in the house would die and the baby had to go too.

Now I go into the kids room. They're both asleep in the same bed. I stand there for awhile watching them sleep. I feel a tremendous rush knowing that soon I will molest them and kill them.

I walk over to the bed and pull down the covers. I reach down to play with the boys penis when I notice he's wet the bed. Now my rush is almost too much to handle. I start playing with his penis and he wakes up and starts crying for his Mom. His sister wakes up and starts crying too. I tell them that I killed their Mom and Dad. I tell them if they don't do whatever I say that I'll kill them too. I flash my knife at them. They beg me not to hurt them. Their fear only feeds my excitement and I try to think of ways to make them more afraid.

Now I take off my clothes and put on a condom. I rub the boys underpants all over my face while I make them do oral sex on each other. Then I make the girl put my penis in her mouth. She tries to get away and I tell her I'm going show her what happens to little girls who don't do what I tell them to. I get some dental floss from my bag and tie her hands to the headboard of the bed. She's on her stomach. I then tie her legs to the footboard. From my bag I pull out a belt and proceed to beat her butt and legs until they have red welts all over them. My excitement is almost unbearable now. I turn her over and rape her.

During my time with his sister the boy has been crouched in a corner. His eyes are glassy and he looks like he's in a trance or something. I untie the girl and tell her to put my penis in her mouth. This time she complies. I tell the boy to come over to the bed. I lift him up and place him on me so I can give him oral sex while his sister has my penis in her mouth.

When I get ready to come I throw the boy off me and push the girls head all the way down on me. She choking and squirming but I don't care, Her pain and fear only feed my excitement. When I finish I put on a new condom and make the boy perform oral sex on me while I finger fuck the girl. After I come I tie up the boy with the dental floss and whip his butt and legs until they're red and swollen. He's screaming from the pain but I don't care. I lick his ass then I put my penis in it. While I'm doing this I have the girl lay on the bed while I perform oral sex on her.

When I'm done with them I make them douche with the bag I brought with me. I make them brush their teeth. Now I stab them numerous times with my knife.

Now that it's over I realize I'm hungry so I go to the kitchen and fix myself a sandwich. I clean up my sandwich mess and go into the bathroom to take a shower. When I'm done I get dressed and take out the video recorder that I brought along and proceed to film the bodies of my victims. Finally I gather all my stuff and leave.

In my fantasy I mail the video tape to the media with a note saying "the fault lies with the system that releases a known child molester without proper treatment. You guys knew what I was but you refused to keep me away from kids. You refused to give me the treatment I needed. You're responsible for what I did as much, no, more than me."

verse:one)   A "MIND FOR ▓▓ MURDER"

1) I'm in that state of ▓▓ mind
2) For slaughterin' up a 1000 mutha-fuckas at a time
3) I gotta feel a taste for bloody flesh ▓▓▓▓▓▓
                                this schizo pahrenic killa
4) No! No! I'm not insane but bitch I wouldn't give ah
5) Fuck about you sluts it's best to step-up out my path
6) Or you gone be the victims of this red river blood bath
7) Watch this nigga fuck yo world around and leave a panic
8) If I could kill enough of you I'd have a red Atlantic
9) Ocean in this mutha-fucka yeah this fool forreal
10) I gotta quench I gotta grunch and its my thirst through
     yo blood spill
11) An empty-hearted sycho pathic nigga with the screws
12) Thinkin' of leavin' whole families drowned in a swimming pool
13) MURDER! No need to kill yaself give me the pleasure
14) The honor! The privelege! I take it all together
15) Yes I love what I do and bitch I do it with perfection
16) Just A MIND FOR THE MURDER gives me love and
     effection

(verse : two)   "A MIND FOR MURDER"

) I gotta problem you dig
) Gotta roll to the farm station slice me a pig
) For the feast get them po-po's up off my track
) Let's pretend they the lambs I'm the wolf in the pack
) My intention, Is blowin' up the whole fuckin' station
) The biggest bloodstain in the mutha-fuckin' nation
) What I think about you ho's is really nothing none the less
) What I need is to kill ~~slappin'~~ plugs out yo chest
) What I feel is to live to see the lost of yo blood
) Just chop off the neck and watch you wiggle in the mud
) Death, kill, murder, slaughter, knock they all mean the same
) For the goal that I ache foe just one aim
) Chill ! Together we assist
) I know he would just rather watch yo body burn to crisp
) With this mix I know you tramps won't make it through the
   night
) It's just "A MIND FOR the MURDER" when it comes out right

HEAD LINES — HEAD LINES — HEAD LINES — 9-9-96

HEAR-YE HEAR-YE — PROBLEM IN 2-A ....
BLACK ON WHITE CRIME IN OUR WING TODAY.
MAN GET ASSULTED — ITS RULE #2 ....
NO ONE WAS CAUGHT — WHAT YOU GOING TO DO?
THIS IS A PROBLEM — ONE YOU CAN NOT SEE ...
YOU CANT STOP PROBLEMS — WHILE SITTING IN YOUR TREE.
SEND ONE OFFICER — TO JUST KINDA LOOK AROUND ....
HAVE HIM MIX LIKE A CAT — TRUTH WILL BE FOUND.
TO LOCK DOWN THE WING — WOULD CREATE MORE TROUBLE ...
SOME THINGS CANT BE SEEN — BY OFFICERS SITTING IN THE BUBBL
TRY TO HANDLE THIS — IN ANY OTHER WAY ...
YOU WILL BUILD MORE PRESSURE — TO EXPLODE ANOTHER DAY.
MAYBE FOR A CASEWORKER — TO HAVE ALL TO SIGN ....
DO AS SUGGESTED — ARE YOU CREATE MORE CRIME.
IF YOU CALL ALL INMATES — TO CENTER OF THE WING ...
COUNT ALL HEADS — NO ONE SUSPECTS A THING.
MAKE THE EXCUSE — YOU WANT TO TALK ABOUT THE 7:00 LOCKUP TIME.
HEED MY WARNING OR BLACKS ATTACKS MORE WHITES IN CRIME.
YOU KNOW NOT ALL WHITES ARE STRONG AND BOLD ...
SO HANDLE THIS CORRECTLY TO PROTECT THE WEAK AND OLD.
KEEP THIS POEM WITH CONTENTS FOR JUST THE TOP STAFF ...
TO MANY INVOLVED WILL NOT MAKE GOOD MATH.
SOME OF YOUR OFFICERS GIVE UP TO MUCH WITH TALK ...
SO HANDLE WITH CARE FOR THE WEAK MUST LIVE ON THE WALK.
MAKE SURE NOT TO LOOK GUILTY WHILE LOOKING FOR PREY ....
MAKE IT LOOK LIKE YOU STUMBLED ON BY CHANCE IN SOME WAY.
THIS WAY YOU WILL NOT HAVE TO LOCK DOWN THE WING ...
NO ONE IS FRONTED OFF — WHILE YOU MAKE YOUR STING.
THE BLACK MAN SHOULD LEAVE GET MOVED — HE IS YOUR MAN ....
HE ASSULTED WHITE MAN — WITH MORE THEN HIS HAND.
<— TURN OVER —>

PAGE TWO

TAKE HIM OUT WHEN HE IS FOUND — AWAY FROM HIS MOURFIED BROTHER
FOR THE REASON IS IT WAS BLACKS THAT KEPT HIM COVERED.
REMEMBER TO ACT LIKE YOU JUST STUMBLED UP ON IT....
OR TENTION CONTINUES TO BUILD AND YOU WONT SOLVE SHIT.
THEN PUT A OFFICER AT THE DESK INSIDE THE P.C. WING.
REMEMBER PROTECTION IS THE KEY TO THIS THING.
REMOVE THE BLACK MAN AS SOON AS HE'S FOUND — FAR-FAST-FAR-AWAY.
NO MORE WEAK WHITES IN P.C. WILL END UP HIS PREY.

POET UNKNOWN.

WHAT YA GUNNA DO — LET THEM CONTINUE?

978-0-595-33457-5
0-595-33457-1